D1130651

Shakespeare's Women

ANGELA PITT

Shakespeare's Women

DAVID & CHARLES
Newton Abbot London

BARNES & NOBLE BOOKS
Totowa, New Jersey

To Tricia

British Library Cataloguing in Publication Data

Pitt, Angela
  Shakespeare's women.
  1. Shakespeare, William – Characters – Women
  2. Women in literature
  I. Title
  822.3'3   PR2991

ISBN 0 7153 7848 1

ISBN 0–389–20122–7 (United States)

Photoset, printed in Great Britain
by Redwood Burn Limited, Trowbridge & Esher
for David & Charles (Publishers) Limited
Brunel House Newton Abbot Devon

First published in the USA 1981 by
Barnes & Noble Books
81 Adams Drive
Totowa, New Jersey, 07512

Contents

Introduction

'Thousands and thousands of books have been written about Shakespeare, and most of them are mad,' wrote a distinguished critic[1] in the 1930s. To this startling revelation could have been added the fact that not one of these books contained a comprehensive study of the women in Shakespeare's plays, an omission that should indeed have merited the charge of insanity. Even now, nearly half a century later, despite the fascination that Shakespeare continues to hold for authors and readers, there is still no book exclusively devoted to his women. Some authors (notably Frank Harris in *The Women of Shakespeare* and Ivor Brown in *The Women in Shakespeare's Life*) have selected female characters from the plays for discussion, but only as illustrations to support their theories about Shakespeare's own life. Other books and articles have focused on a group of the plays or heroines for close academic analysis.

The present book represents an attempt to fill the gap between the two, and is not intended for the Shakespeare-specialist. It seeks first to explore the attitudes towards women current in Shakespeare's time, and then to examine the various female roles in the plays, bearing these attitudes in mind. It also traces the history of Shakespeare's women on stage.

There is a great temptation to see Shakespeare's heroines as reflections of the women among his friends and family, and then to take the next step and create a biography based on the plays. It is highly likely that Shakespeare did base his characters (and not just the women) on people he knew, but how can we tell who, when and where? What we do know from the evidence of the plays themselves is that he had an extraordinarily subtle mind and a seemingly boundless imagination. It is crassly naïve to suppose that a man with such creative gifts would, of necessity, transpose his day-to-day life and relationships directly into his plays. It may well be that we glimpse his daughters in Perdita or Miranda, his wife in Adriana and his mother in Volumnia, but seizing on such resemblances is the result of speculation alone and ultimately can only obstruct our view.

The only factual information we have about the women Shakespeare knew comes from the records of birth, deaths, marriages and legal transactions. Even these can pose problems. We know that Shakespeare married Anne Hathaway, but the event is not recorded in the parish register. Instead we find that the Bishop of Worcester granted a special licence for William Shakespeare to marry Anne Whately on 27 November 1582. In records for the following day a bond of £40 is said to have provided for Shakespeare's marriage, but this time the

[1] Logan Pearsall Smith.

woman's name is Anne Hathaway. Some scholars claim that the confusion results simply from the local clerk muddling up the names and that Anne Whately either never existed or else had no connection with Shakespeare. It does seem rather a major error to make, however, particularly as the clerk also wrote that she came from Temple Grafton, a place-name difficult to confuse with Stratford, Anne Hathaway's home. As it is likely that Shakespeare's marriage was hastened or even forced by Anne Hathaway's pregnancy (she gave birth to their daughter Susanna barely six months later), there is also the theory that Shakespeare tried to marry the mysterious Anne Whately but was prevented by the Hathaway family. Ingenious arguments have been advanced on both sides, but the truth remains elusive

Other information about women Shakespeare knew comes from chance remarks by his contemporaries, but it is difficult to know how much weight can be placed on them. An example is an entry in the diary for 1602 of one John Manningham. He refers to an incident which took place when the good looks of Richard Burbage, who was playing Richard III, so attracted a woman in the audience that before she left the theatre she arranged to meet him later that night. He was to bang on her door and say he was Richard III. Shakespeare overheard the plan and got to her first. He was 'at his game ere Burbidge came. Then message being brought that Rich. the 3d was at the dore Shakespeare caused returne to be made that William the Conqueror was before Richard the 3'. It is an amusing story with a good punch-line, which is no doubt why Manningham bothered to record it. How true it is, is another matter! By 1602 Shakespeare was already quite a well-known and probably envied figure and therefore likely to be the butt of a few scurrilous jokes and anecdotes. Manningham's story sounds a little too pat to be true, an Elizabethan version of those present-day jokes that begin with the formula: 'Do you know the one about . . .?'

Such tales apart, it is not too difficult to piece together the facts we have about Shakespeare, his mother, wife, daughters, niece and granddaughter, but what we cannot tell from the parish registers is the quality of his relationships with these women. Neither, of course, is any mistress recorded there, or anywhere else for that matter, although this has not deterred many of Shakespeare's biographers from assuming he had one, and attempting to prove her identity. Their arguments invariably rest on what they decipher from that extraordinary sequence of one hundred and fifty-four poems: the sonnets.

Because of their candid tone the sonnets sound as though they chronicle a series of personal revelations, and they have been used by generations of readers as a potential mine of information about Shakespeare's private life. If the information is indeed there, it is very well hidden, for the sonnets are fraught with ambiguities and mysteries. We do not know when most of them were written, whom they address, or even to whom the complete collection was dedicated. What we do know is that to write poignantly about matters of the heart in sonnet-form was as much a literary convention in Elizabethan England as the stylisation of love and lovers in a pastoral poem with its nymphs and shepherds. Reading the sonnets from a standpoint in the twentieth century, when such conscious conventions in poetry seem artificial and are alien to our taste, it is easy to assume that because Shakespeare writes so movingly and directly, the situations, people and feelings in these poems are 'real'. It may well be that what we are witnessing in the best of the sonnets is Shakespeare at the height of his art, creating the supreme dramatic illusion for his readers: the illusion that we can see directly into his heart and mind.

Scholars who believe that the sonnets are autobiographical are frequently at pains to identify the man who is addressed in many of the first one hundred and twenty-six poems and the Dark Lady of the remainder. Inevitably, perhaps, some writers have seen the lady as the mysterious Anne Whately, but there is no evidence to support their claim. Neither can the sonnets be used to prove that Shakespeare was exclusively heterosexual, although most of his biographers make a point of stressing that the sensual language in many of those addressed to another man is explicable as a convention of the time. It is a curious but persistent example of double-thinking that whereas the sonnets addressed to the Dark Lady are usually accepted at face-value, as the proof of a traumatic love affair, those that speak of yearning for a man's love are rapidly explained away as conventional gestures of friendship or loyalty or a desire for patronage. In all probability this is indeed the case, but it cannot be *proved* from the sonnets. Another factor is that a large number of these poems could have been addressed either to a man or a woman, but are invariably taken by readers as intended for the Dark Lady because this fulfils their own expectations of Shakespeare.

In the present book no attempt has been made to extract biographical information from the sonnets because of the perils and ambiguities they present. The focus is on the women in the plays, women more real to us than Anne Hathaway or Susanna and Judith, women whose grace, caprice, dignity and power has brought them alive for each generation of play-goers: Shakespeare's women.

I

The Historical Setting
for Shakespeare's Women

England is a woman's paradise, a servant's
prison and a horse's hell.

Sixteenth century proverb

With some surprise, and perhaps even a hint of censure, the Duke of
Württemberg, visiting England in 1602, noted that, 'the women have
much more liberty than perhaps in any other place'. It is the word
'liberty' that trumpets out from his remark. What kind of freedom does
he mean? Can it be, that in England at least, there was a working notion
of Renaissance Woman to parallel the concept of that fortunate demi-
god, Renaissance Man? At its most narrow level of interpretation
'liberty', or rather 'more liberty', seems to imply that Elizabethan
women had some considerable measure of independence and a sense of
their own identity compared with their sisters across the channel.

Württemberg's statement is frustratingly provocative as it stands,
but serves as an excellent flame to kindle discussion of the real position of
women in both Elizabethan and Jacobean England. Without such
consideration of their living counterparts it would be ludicrous to
attempt a just description and analysis of the women in Shakespeare's
plays. No matter how subtly his characters are evolved in psychological
and literary terms so that they seem magically 'contemporary' to any
reader in any age, their creation is still firmly rooted in the years between
1588 and 1613. Shakespeare did not write in a social vacuum. His
livelihood depended on his audience being pleased, and his audience
would have given short shrift to plays whose characters were hopelessly
out of keeping with current attitudes. It is worth remembering that
Shakespeare's audiences were notoriously unruly. If they did not enjoy a
play they would hiss and 'mew' at the actors, crack nuts on the floor and
probably end up noisily drunk, completely disrupting the performance.
The 'groundlings', who had the cheapest tickets and stood in the bottom

1 The hint of wilfulness and capricious humour in her expression suggests that this un-identified sixteenth-century woman had a mind of her own

gallery of the theatre, were the worst offenders and were termed 'penny stinkards' by a contemporary courtier. Stinkards or not, they were powerful arbiters, and no theatre-owner would dare persist with performances of a play that they found boring. Most of Shakespeare's plays were popular in his own lifetime. This was not because the audiences realised they were watching the works of a genius, but for the more down-to-earth reason that he captured their imaginations by showing them the personalities of their friends, their wives, their mistresses, their husbands and lovers, and themselves. The outward shape of Shakespeare's characters might well be that of kings and queens, and the plays themselves set in foreign lands, but the relationships and reactions evolved were totally comprehensible to the Elizabethan play-goer who might never have rubbed shoulders with the aristocracy nor been closer to the Continent than the south bank of the Thames.

To understand both the conception and full impact of Shakespeare's female characters it is therefore crucial to see them in their historical setting. The Duke of Württemberg can help us.

It had become fashionable in the late sixteenth century for continental gentlemen, particularly Germans, to consider a visit to England as indispensable to the rounding off of their education. Such visits appear to have taken the form of a fairly standardised package-tour, which would cover the sights of London and might be extended to include a brief visit to Oxford or Cambridge. A detailed journal of sights seen and eccentricities observed was often kept, presumably for subsequent reading at home by incredulous friends and relatives. Some of these journals have survived, and although their contents often sound so similar as to suggest that it is the words of a paid English guide that are recorded rather than the personal observations of the diarist, they must, in essence at least, be true. There would be no reason for traveller after traveller to report the same snippets of information if contrary evidence presented itself.

In keeping with this continuity, the Duke of Württemberg's comment on women is an echo of similar remarks made three years earlier in 1599 by Thomas Platter of Basel. He writes that women 'have far more liberty than in other lands and know just how to make good use of it'. He adds that English men have to put up with their wives' behaviour, for if they protest, their wives will beat them! This may well be a piece of jocular national chauvinism on Platter's part, to assert the superior, vigorous masculinity of his own countrymen who were famed for keeping their

2 The Elizabethan citizen's wife had some measure of independence for she could enjoy such diversions as a visit to the theatre or the tavern without her husband

women under control, but one cannot dismiss so lightly his more specific remarks on English social behaviour. He tells us that women are frequently seen at the plays, bear-baiting and cock fights, and also:

> What is particularly curious is that the women as well as the men, in fact more often than they, will frequent the taverns or ale-houses for enjoyment. They count it a great honour to be taken there and given wine with sugar to drink; and if one woman only is invited, then she will bring three or four other women along and they gaily toast each other.

The close attention to detail (the sugared wine) and the lively picture he presents of women drinking each other's healths are unique among such tourist-journals and must spring from personal observation. It is not prostitutes, whom no man would have been surprised to find in an ale-house, but ordinary middle-class women who are meant here. They would be wives of city tradesmen or merchants, and it is interesting to

12

3 Whether a humble country-woman like this or a lady at court, a woman was legally her husband's property

note that it was socially acceptable for such women to go to taverns at all, let alone without a man. Platter evidently found it surprising, and had another shock when he went to eat with an old friend of his, a theologian. He discovered that 'in England it is not customary to invite a man without his wife', and so the wife came too.

From the shape of Platter's comments we can see that he is taking his homeland as the norm and, like any tourist, picking out anything at variance with it to store up for telling his inquisitive friends when he got back. Typical of such curiosities are the odd collection of animals belonging to the Queen which he saw in the Tower of London: six lions, a lioness, a wolf, a tiger and a porcupine. Almost as if to prove he was there, Platter adds that a lion tried to claw one of his servants through the bars of its cage. Personal anecdotes of this kind give his journal entries a lively immediacy, whether writing of the habits of Elizabeth's lions or English women, but we must be wary of placing too much importance on them.

Platter, Württemberg and other travellers give us fascinating glimpses of Elizabethan life, including Elizabethan women, but seen through continental eyes and contrasted with continental standards. The last thing these tourists intended was to make profound social judgements. To see if the 'liberty' they mention for Elizabethan women does in fact point to fundamental freedoms and rights we need to consult different sources. For women to have meaningful rights they would need to be stated in the laws of the land, the doctrines of the church and shown in the practices of the time.

Elizabethan law offers no general statement on the position of women. There is no text or statute specifically concerned with their rights—or lack of them. It is only from references to the woman's place under laws governing such areas as marriage, inheritance and tenure that we can determine her legal position. At first glance the women appear to have had a surprisingly good deal. While unmarried they had virtually all the rights of a man. But the catch lies in the word 'unmarried'. In practice it was virtually impossible for a woman (unless she was Queen of England!) to remain unmarried and independent. Marriages were still arranged, as they had been in the Middle Ages, to further the interests of land-owning families. On marriage all the girl's legal rights ceased and she became as much the property of her husband as his horse or barn. Concern about this contractual, property-owning side of marriage, particularly as it affects the girl's father and the prospective suitors, occurs in some of Shakespeare's plays, notably *The Merchant of Venice*. It is interesting also to look at Katharina's long speech in *The Taming of the Shrew* when she has finally been subdued by Petruchio. Here she voices the 'correct' attitude of a wife:

> Such duty as the subject owes the prince,
> Even such, a woman oweth to her husband;
> And when she is froward, peevish, sullen, sour,
> And not obedient to his honest will,
> What is she but a foul contending rebel,
> And graceless traitor to her loving lord?

(V.ii 153–8)

Although some husbands broke with medieval conventions and allowed their wives to take part in running businesses (such as printing and bookselling) or to join a Guild, this did not give the wives any kind of legal independence. No doubt they gained confidence and a greater sense of personal identity through being allowed out of the traditional

14

sphere of the house, but they were still their husbands' chattels.

If for some reason it was impractical for a girl to marry—there might be insufficient dowry if there were several daughters in the family—she was encouraged to enter a nunnery. On entry, all her possessions were made over to the religious house and she lost all secular rights.

The only time a woman might be able to wield some influence was if her husband died and she was left in charge either of a business (like Mistress Quickly who runs the Boar's Head Tavern in *King Henry IV, Parts 1 and 2* and *King Henry V*) or of the family estates. Francis Bacon's mother, Lady Anne Bacon, was just such a tough, formidable old woman. Francis got into debt and asked his mother to sell off some land in order to pay his bills. She sent him a tartly-worded letter demanding a precise list of the debts before she would proceed with the sale. He was obliged to provide it for her, even though he was thirty years old and a Member of Parliament! Her counterpart in Shakespeare must surely be Volumnia, the powerful, possessive mother of Coriolanus.

In the eyes of the law then, a woman was theoretically the equal of a man. But in practice, most women were never able to wield any significant legal or political power because they 'belonged' either to a man or to the Church.

The Church was immensely influential in shaping society's expectations of women. To understand something of Elizabethan ecclesiastical attitudes, we need to look back through the 1500s to the beginnings of Protestant Reform.

Elizabeth's father, Henry VIII, had made himself head of the Church in England. This meant that for the first time in English history, the monarch could, if he wished, dictate church policy to his bishops. Predictably, there were many changes brought about. Some affected the wealth and influence of the Church (Henry VIII seized land, plate and money to pay royal bills); others affected Church doctrine (reformed under Edward VI); yet others affected the basic sectarian nature of the Church (Mary attempted the forceful restoration of Roman Catholicism). At no time, however, did any monarch attempt to change or even question the Church's attitude towards women. This attitude was the same one that had been doggedly maintained throughout the Middle Ages: women were the daughters of Eve, temptresses who would lead men down the primrose path to fornication. Their women's bodies proclaimed that they were the living symbols of Man's First Disgrace. Everyone knew that, because it was not only in the Book of Genesis, but in the New Testament where St Paul spoke of women as being inferior to

4 Shakespeare created a forceful intellectual in Portia, here portrayed by Fay Davis, in 1909

men. Early Church Fathers, such as St Jerome, enlarged on the subject of women's inferiority with a misogynist vengeance. Their views, reinforced by the authority of the scriptures, became accepted as 'fact' by both men and women alike. The official ecclesiastical view, up to and well beyond Elizabeth's reign, was that man represented the supreme height of God's creation, while woman was secondary, inferior to him in every way. This was the official view, but we have only to look at the strong, respected figure of Elizabeth herself and the lively heroines in Shakespeare's plays to know that there must be another side to the social picture.

Although the English monarchs were not concerned with the position of women, Protestant reformers were. First of all, throughout the sixteenth century there is a growing emphasis on the importance of marriage, thus breaking with the medieval ideal of virginity. This meant that some elements of the Church at least were preaching that a woman's role as wife and mother was as good as, or even superior to, the cloistered purity of the nun. Spiritual status was thus given to marriage and society was encouraged to view women more seriously. The very fact that the position of women was under discussion in the Church represented a huge leap away from the rigid attitudes of the previous century.

A more exciting and ultimately significant development however, was the demand for education for women. This grew out of the principles and activities of a devout group of intellectuals and religious idealists: the Humanists.

In the early 1500s Erasmus visited his fellow Humanist, Thomas More, in England. He was much impressed by the running of More's household and particularly by his friend's insistence on an education for his daughters. The idea that girls should be educated sprang from the Humanist belief that exalted character can come only as a result of education. Erasmus agreed with More that it was actually sinful not to educate the young. Otherwise they would not be well equipped to meet temptations or recognise evil. The Humanists did not, however, see girls and boys as equal. Their concept of education was founded on the old medieval premise that women were the weaker sex, but they gave it a new twist. Their idea was that since women are more frivolous and less stable than men, it is *crucial* that they be educated in order to fortify them sufficiently to cope with their inherent deficiencies. Education for girls was thus seen as an effective preventative medicine, and the Humanists were working towards spiritual, not social ends.

Nevertheless, there were far-reaching social consequences. The kind of education which Thomas More envisaged for his daughters was provided by private tuition, and he set a fashion for girls from rich bourgeois, as well as aristocratic, families to learn foreign languages and study the Scriptures. Soon the daughters from such homes were learning Latin, Greek and even Hebrew. This is reflected in Shakespeare's plays, for his heroines come from aristocratic or wealthy homes, and their spirited speeches often reveal the learning deemed appropriate for such women. For example, Beatrice shows a fair knowledge of geography and history in *Much Ado About Nothing*, Rosalind (*As You Like It*) is able to cite

5 Like most of Shakespeare's heroines, Celia and Rosalind came from a wealthy aristo-cratic background where women were expected to have some measure of academic edu-cation. Rosalind is played by Dorothy Tutin and Celia by Janet Suzman

classical myths and Helena (*A Midsummer Night's Dream*) mentions her 'school-days' friendship' with Hermia.

It was however believed that girls should read only 'suitable' books, and strict censorship was expected of the tutor. In a book of rules for parents and 'scholemaisters', 1594, Edward Hake was vocal on the subject of what happens if a girl is allowed to read what she likes:

> Eyther shee is altogither kept from exercises of good learning and knowledge of good letters or else she is so nouseled in amourous bookes, vain stories, and fonde trifling fancies that she smelleth of naughtinesse even all hir lyfe after.

In the same year Thomas Salter produced his *Mirrhor of Modestie* expressly to encourage girls to read only what would not tax their intellects or excite their fantasies. He attacks 'lascivious ballades' and recommends that no girl should be allowed to read love stories, even classical ones such as that of Dido and Æneas. He particularly condemns as unsuitable the 'filthie' (i.e., homosexual) love indulged in by the Greek poets. A girl, says Salter, should spend her time reading

Christian books and the lives of good women. It will, after all, be her duty to read the Bible to her children. Another writer suggests that if girls become entranced by love stories, there will be dire results:

> Love of the beauty is a forgetting of reason, and the nexte thynge unto fransy, a foule vice and an unmannerly for an hole mynde, it troubleth al the wyttes, it breaketh and abateth hygh and noble stomackes, and draweth them down from the study and thynkyng of high and excellente thinges unto lowe and vile and causeth them to be ful of gronyng . . .

Not all the girls listened to the learned men. By the late 1500s a mass of love poetry and romances was produced, evidently to satisfy the tastes of a female readership. Neither must we forget that women were among the audience in the play-houses. Shakespeare was certainly aware of their presence and in the Epilogue to *As You Like It*, Rosalind addresses them:

> I charge you, O women, for the love you bear to men, to like as much of this play as please you . . .

Literacy and the little learning that girls had must have proved both a boon and a frustration. Since her place in life was to be a good wife to her husband, raise his children and look after his house, a girl was not encouraged to grow up with the idea that she would have the leisure for philosophy. Neither was she suited (because of her fundamentally weak mind) to be a lawyer, physician or preacher. The sixteenth-century ideal for the educated woman shows an interesting mixture of the kind of skills her great-grandmother would have been expected to master (neat handwriting, clear reading aloud, dancing, singing, drawing, embroidery and housekeeping) and those approved by the Humanists (a knowledge of one or two modern languages, the classical languages, and a smattering of logic and rhetoric). Some ladies became true scholars. The Countess of Pembroke, sister of the poet Sir Philip Sidney, was praised by her contemporaries for her translation of a lengthy French work. But not all women had the same opportunities as the Countess of Pembroke. Once married and busy from dawn to dusk with household matters, they had no time to pursue more demanding studies but could find an escape through reading romantic fiction. The literary establishment was sharply critical both of these supposedly self-indulgent women and of those who wrote for them. Here is a

6 A mid-sixteenth-century portrait, possibly of Lady Jane Grey. Such young women from aristocratic circles were literate and some authors wrote with an eye to pleasing their tastes

contemporary of Shakespeare's, Thomas Nashe, sneering at such writers.

> Many of them, to be more amiable with their friends of the Feminine sexe, blot many sheetes of paper in the blazing of Women's slender praises, as though in that generation there raigned and alwaies remained such singuler simplicitie that all posterities should be injoyed by duetie, to fill and furnish theyr Temples, nay Townes and streetes, with the shrines of the saints.

Not all men offered such restrictive guidelines or were as censorious as these. The influential Elizabethan writer, Richard Mulcaster, defends the theory of education for women. He says:

> We see yong maidens be taught to read and write, and can do both passing well; we know that they learne the best and finest of our learned languages, to the admiration of all men.

He adds the positive assertion: 'myself am for them tooth and nail.'

Women themselves could be defensive about what they no doubt were conditioned to believe was bold entry into masculine territory. When Margaret Tyler brought out a scholarly translation in 1578 she forestalled possible attack by saying in her preface that such work was not 'unseemely for a woman to deale in'. Signs of independence in a girl were certainly resented. In his will of 1558, Michael Wentworth warns his five daughters that if any of them go against the wishes of his executors and

> of their awne fantastical brayne bestow themselves lightly upon a light personne thenne I will that daughter to have but one hundred marcs.

The problem of what was seemly or unseemly for women certainly concerned Juan Vives, staunch Roman Catholic and religious adviser to Catherine of Aragon. He wrote a treatise for her, which its English translator termed 'A very Fruteful and Pleasant boke callyd the Instruction of a Christen woman'. The Christian woman in Vives' view should be principally concerned with 'the ornament of her soul, and the keeping and ordering of an house'. He then addresses his woman reader directly, instructing her not to become embroiled in politics or government: 'Your own house is a city great enough for you.' Catherine of Aragon presumably accepted the warning meekly enough, but it is easy to see from this and other similar remarks why Vives' manual dropped out of circulation once Elizabeth came to the throne!

Most of Vives' opinions derived directly from the medieval tradition, but it is interesting that even he, with his ultra-conservative background of Spanish Catholicism, shows that Humanist ideas have affected him. On the one hand he is prepared to state the old slogan that learning for women would 'be a nourishment for the maliciousness of their nature'. On the other, he concedes elsewhere in the book that:

> This [lack of education] is the only reason why all women for the most part are hard to please, studious and most diligent to adorn themselves, marvellers of trifles, in prosperity proud and insolent; and for lack of good learning, they love and hate that only the which they learned of their unlearned mothers.

Although the Humanist influence is almost hidden amongst Vives' exhortations to women to be submissive and concern themselves only with house and husband, other writers were unable to reconcile the two. Thomas More and the other Humanists had unwittingly started the sparks flying when they promoted the idea of education for women. Literary and academic arguments crackled on the pages of authors both in England and on the continent throughout the sixteenth and well into the seventeenth century. This preoccupation with women's capabilities is known as *La Querelle des Femmes* (the dispute about women).

Those supporting the women too often wrote long lists of their 'virtues' (grace, meekness and submission), which make tedious reading and have little real relevance to the issue of education. Presumably they were intended to reassure the opposition that there was no *real* problem. On the same superficial level, though supporting the other side, are the satirical portraits of women in plays like *The Two Angry Women of Abington*, 1598, in which the husbands are shamed by their scolding wives; a literary tradition that had its origins in the Middle Ages. Some writers with considerable temerity, although perhaps only for argument's sake, claimed that women were actually *superior* to men. Such provocation raised a howl of protest from the pulpit and other supporters of the official Church view. Some dug up the old Aristotelian theory that a women was a deformity of man. Others invoked the authority of the Bible. Here is the fiery Scot, preacher and misogynist, John Knox, sounding off in *The First Blast of the Trumpet against the Monstrous Regiment of Women*, 1558:

> The holy ghost doth manifestly [say]: I suffer not that women usurp authority over men: he sayeth not, that woman usurp authority over her husband, but he nameth man in general, taking from her all power and

7 Catherine of Aragon, the ill-fated first wife of Henry VIII, here portrayed by Dame Peggy Ashcroft, in 1969

authority, to speak, to reason, to interpret or to teach, but principally to rule or to judge in the assembly of men. So that woman by the law of God and the interpretation of the holy ghost is utterly forbidden to occupy the place of God in the offices aforesaid, which he hath assigned to man, whom he hath appointed and ordained his lieutenant in earth: secluding from that honour and dignity all women.... And therefore yet again I repeat that, which I have affirmed: to wit, that a woman promoted to sit in the seat of God, that is to teach, to judge, or to reign above man, is a monster in nature, contumely to God, and a thing most repugnant to his will and ordinance.

The principle object of this vitriolic diatribe was Mary Tudor, but Knox was citing and dramatising all the old religious arguments against woman that seek to establish her fundamental inferiority to man. As such, the popularity of *The First Blast of the Trumpet* long outlived its author, for while it was, no doubt, only quoted in whispers while Elizabeth was queen, its sentiments won open approval from her successor, James I.

Some diehards went further than Knox and claimed that women belonged to a different species altogether! The war of words finally petered out in the seventeenth century, by which time the original issues had become obscured. In spite of being so academic, the issue had obvious social repercussions for women. It forced attention, however negative, to be paid to their position and society's expectations of them.

A more lasting development was the increase throughout the sixteenth century of schools where girls might be taught, together with boys (as in Christ's Hospital, founded in 1555). One is reminded of Holofernes' boarding school in *Love's Labours Lost*, which took both boys and girls. There were also schools especially for girls. Many of these were founded by Protestants escaping persecution in Europe, and were in addition to, or even in competition with, the few nunneries left open after the Dissolution. These nunneries would educate girls, for a small fee, in the basic skills, music, sewing and rudimentary French (just such an education is envisaged for Bianca in *The Taming of the Shrew*). The Protestant schools placed rather more emphasis on book learning, but even so, they did not offer education to much beyond what we would term primary-school level. In order to progress beyond this stage, a girl would have to go on to a grammar school and be taught alongside her brothers. Few girls were encouraged to do so, not just because by the age of thirteen or fourteen they could be safely married off, but because education in the grammar school was basically designed to train boys to be parsons, and thus it had little relevance to the needs of girls. Once she

24

Margaret Russell Countesse
of Cumberland. 1588:

8 Inspired by the example of her Queen, Margaret Russell, the Countess of Cumberland, was one of a number of wealthy ladies who patronised the arts and learning in the Elizabethan age

Qui voudra figurer, d'vn ouurage parfect,
La beauté, la Vertu, l'Ornement, et les graces,
De Nature, des Dieux, de l'vniuers, des Graces,
A œoure contempler la grand'ELIZABETH.

9 The flattering words in this frontispiece to a poem in 1586 came close to reality, for as a patroness of the arts the Queen far outshone any of her contemporaries. ('He who wishes to make a perfect composition of the beauty, virtue, adornment and favours of Nature, the gods, the universe and the Graces, should hurry to view the great Elizabeth.')

could master basic arithmetic, the ABC, the Lord's Prayer and simple sentences a girl could leave school. For some this meant no formal education beyond the age of nine. She would then be sufficiently numerate and literate to cope with domestic accounts and perhaps to improve her housekeeping and other practical skills by reading some of many do-it-yourself-type manuals produced for women at that time. These included books on needlework, cookery, lace-making, herbs and medicines.

In view of the existence of cheap elementary education for girls it is inaccurate to think that girls from families who could not afford private tutors had no school training at all. We learn from Sir Thomas Overbury's book of 'characters' (published in 1614) that even servants might be literate. He says of a chamber-maid that 'she reads Greene's works over and over and is so carried away with the *Mirror of Knighthood* that she is many times resolved to remain one herself and become a Lady Errant'. In Shakespeare's *The Merry Wives of Windsor*, both Mistress Ford and Mistress Page, ordinary townswomen, are able to read Falstaff's letter. Literacy was evidently neither a masculine nor an aristocratic monopoly.

By the time of Elizabeth, then, there were two types of 'educated' women. First, there were those who were simply literate and whose schooling had ended at an early age. Second, there were the daughters of the rich or the principled whose scholastic training could well approach that of their brothers. The outstanding woman among these great ladies, both in rank and accomplishment, was, of course, the Queen herself.

Elizabeth was remarkable. From an early age she showed great intellectual curiosity and her aptitude for study was encouraged by her step-mother Katherine Parr. By the age of eleven Elizabeth was even able to write in fluent Italian, as witnessed by a letter to her step-mother in 1544. One of the best minds of the age, Roger Ascham, was ultimately engaged as her tutor and by her early adolescence Elizabeth was proficient in an incredible range of subjects: history, geography, mathematics, Latin, Greek, French, Italian, Spanish, Flemish, music, architecture and astronomy. There is some evidence that she even learned Welsh from a Mrs Parry, Keeper of the Royal Books. In addition, she had a deep love of the arts and was renown for her true appreciation of the works of those poets, painters and musicians of whom she was patroness. Roger Ascham wrote of her 'ardent love of true religion and of the best kind of literature. The constitution of her mind is

10 Costume of an Elizabethan noblewoman

exempt from female weakness and she is endued with a masculine power of application . . .' It was the greatest compliment that Ascham could pay her—that her brain was as good as a man's. (It is interesting that even in this century some historians still persist in calling Elizabeth 'masculine' or 'unnatural' as a way of accounting for her brilliant mind.)

Elizabeth set high cultural standards for women and was often cited, by those who supported the cause of education for women, as the most compelling proof of their arguments. Such claims could go only so far however; Elizabeth's significance, not just to her subjects but to herself was not that she was a woman, but that she was Queen of England. Her female form was a disability that had to be suffered as best it could. She made, from time to time, calculated use of her 'womanly wiles' to give her a trump card in her dealings with men. As a woman she was allowed by social custom to use charm and even flirtation in a way that would have been judged unseemly for a male monarch. More frequently her attitude to her womanhood was defiant—getting in first with a sneer to silence likely critics. Nowhere does she use this trick of effacing her femininity with more effect than in the rousing speech to the troops at Tilbury Docks in 1588. The men were waiting, depressed and uneasy, knowing that forces from Spain were approaching steadily in an Armada of a size that could destroy the entire English navy. Elizabeth's passionate words ring out to them, monarch to man:

> I know I have the body of a weak and feeble woman but I have the heart and stomach of a king, and a king of England too, and think foul scorn that Parma and Spain or any Prince of Europe, should dare to invade the borders of my realm.

The effect of the speech comes from qualities that are customarily held to be the best in the masculine tradition: fearless courage, toughness, arrogant defiance and a provocative defence of territory. It is an important aspect of Elizabeth's undoubted greatness as monarch and diplomat that she was able to choose the most appropriate persona for the occasion. By insisting on remaining single and refusing until the very last to name an heir, Elizabeth also showed that a woman could be strong without a man at her side. To many, her decision not to marry appeared unnatural, but whatever her motives, the Queen remained firmly in control and never let her personal advisers or Parliament break her resolve.

As a figurehead, and because her policies in both Church and State tended to the 'middle way', thus setting a standard of judicious compromise and tolerance rather than confrontation, Elizabeth indirectly created a society in which women were more respected and hence more 'free' than they had ever been before. It is this social ease between men and women that must underlie the comments on their 'liberty' by men like Thomas Platter and the Duke of Württemberg. Renaissance goddesses they are not, for the moral ideal for women was still firmly Christian, based on submission and obedience, in contrast with that set up for men, which owes a great deal to the classical figure of the lordly Greek. What they did have was sufficient sense of their importance in society to create unsuppressed vitality in their speech, their actions and their relationships. This was what so impressed the tourists. But it was not to last. Elizabeth's successor had little time for women.

James I was not a pleasant man. His accession in 1603 at first brought relief because the succession question was at last settled, but upsets soon followed. He quarrelled with Parliament and managed to alienate both

Puritans and Catholics. Life in his court became notorious for bribery, drunkenness and immorality. He appears to have been alarmed by women and tried to suppress their 'arrogance' through the clergy. The light of tolerance and respect for women that had begun to burn in Elizabeth's reign was now firmly put out. For example, a Mrs Turner was condemned to death for having dared to invent and parade a frivolous yellow ruff, thus betraying, apparently, her disregard for appropriate behaviour. She was sent to the gallows dressed in the fashion she was said to have invented. Many new treatises on the wickedness of women were published, such as Swetnam's *The Arraignment of Lewd Idle Froward and Unconstant Women*, in 1615. In the same year Tofte's *Blazon of Jealousie* attacks learned women:

> A Woman's Tongue that is as swifte as thought,
> Is ever bad, and she herself starke Nought:
> But she that seldome speakes and mildly then,
> Is a rare Pearle amongst all other Women.
> Maides must be seene, not hearde, or selde or never,
> O may I such one wed, if I wed ever.

Fewer and fewer writers bothered to defend women against such verbal assault. The works of John Knox were reprinted, and both Catholic and Puritan clergy denounced women from the pulpit.

If James was alarmed by women in general, he was terrified of witches in particular. During Elizabeth's reign Reginald Scot had brought out *The Discoverie of Witchcraft*. His express purpose was to contend the reality of witches and force people to see that many of those condemned as being in the devil's power were in fact harmless.

> One sort of such as are said to bee witches, are women which be commonly old, lame, bleare-eied, pale, fowle and full of wrinkles . . .

In other words, any poor old woman. Scot was defending a heresy by questioning the beliefs of his age, but Queen Elizabeth (who certainly believed in witches) ignored his book and its implications, perhaps in order to avoid further publicity for the book. Not so James. As soon as he came to the throne he passed an act against witches and subsequently ordered Scot's book to be burned by the common hangman. During his reign there was much feverish persecution of supposed witches—a constant and sobering reminder to all women that if they appeared in any way eccentric, independent or especially gifted, they might well be

11 King James I. His dislike and fear of women prompted a patronising attitude towards them and harsh policies

12 Costume of a Jacobean
noblewoman

burned at the stake. The best such a woman could expect was ridicule or total lack of comprehension. A Jacobean bluestocking was once presented to the king, but when he heard of her knowledge of Latin, Greek and Hebrew he dismissed these accomplishments with: 'But can she spin?'

Much of what women had achieved in Elizabeth's reign was thus steadily eroded under James, but it is one of those fortunate tricks of history that although Shakespeare wrote plays for some ten years into James's reign, his vision of the women characters remains essentially Elizabethan. He presents many different types of women, but he never moralises, never patronises. The great historian G. M. Trevelyan was moved to say of him:

> More ... can be found out in his plays about the real relations of the two sexes, the position and character of Elizabethan women, than could possibly be expressed in social history.

(English Social History)

II

Shakespeare's Tragic Women

Come down and welcome me to this world's light;
Confer with me of murder and of death.

Titus Andronicus V.ii.33–4

Shakespeare did not take sides in one of the hottest literary issues of his day, the 'dispute about women'. Many of his contemporaries either consistently idealised women in romantic tales and poems, or satirised them as harridans, fools or whores, but Shakespeare scrupulously avoids such two-dimensional stereotyping. This is not to say that he accords them equal status with men, for that would have been too much at variance with their genuine social position to be credible. It was the way in which men and women influence each other and the whole complex sphere of human relationships that intrigued Shakespeare—perhaps above every other consideration. His plays are not vehicles for academic theories and so, although he tacitly accepts the conservative idea of a hierarchy in nature with man at the top and woman second, he does not preach it. This belief in man's unquestioned intrinsic superiority is implied in the plays nevertheless, and in *The Taming of the Shrew* is given voice by Katharina:

Thy husband is thy lord, thy life, thy keper,
Thy head, thy sovereign.

(V.ii.144–5)

In the light of this underlying conviction about a woman's place, it is not surprising to find that Shakespeare's four great tragedies, *King Lear*, *Hamlet*, *Macbeth* and *Othello*, have a tragic hero as their central figure and not a tragic heroine. It is only where tragedy arises from mutual passionate love that the position of the heroine begins to approach the same significance as that of the hero, that is in *Anthony and Cleopatra* and, to a lesser extent, in *Romeo and Juliet*. By its very nature, such love exerts a powerful force over the destinies of *both* parties, thus elevating the woman's position. *Troilus and Cressida*, which is also concerned with the destructive

33

power of passion, does not come into quite the same category. Both hero and heroine remain alive at the end, and the enigma presented by Cressida will be discussed later, separate from the mainstream of the tragedies.

Before considering the characters of Cleopatra and Juliet in greater depth, it is essential to decide what is meant by 'tragic heroine'. Just because a character may die an unfortunate, unpleasant or distressing death does not of itself make her a heroine, or her death a tragic one. It is, however, notoriously difficult to give any water-tight definition of Shakespeare's dramatic method since he left us no statement of his intentions beyond evidence in the plays themselves. An additional problem is that his own notion of 'tragedy' seems to have altered as he grew older and there is thus no set of 'rules' that can be applied to all the plays containing a tragic element, that is, plays ranging from the early historical tragedy *Richard III* through to *Coriolanus*. However, although there is no rigid literary mould for these tragedies and the internal forces that bring catastrophe about are ultimately unique to each play, there are sufficient similarities between the heroes of the four great tragedies for a definition of tragic-quality to be attempted. The cases of Cleopatra and Juliet can then be tested by these criteria since the true nature of tragedy admits no sex-distinction.

The first essential is that the tragic hero must have power and influence so that his fate will affect the condition of more than just his immediate family. Lear and Macbeth are kings, Hamlet is a prince and Othello an important general with political influence. When these men die, the whole fabric of society is shaken, for the calamity is on a vast scale. It is immediately apparent, given the situation in Elizabethan England, that very few women could be imagined in this way, the exception being the woman who, like Cleopatra, was a queen in her own right, not simply the wife of a king.

The second element is the precise nature of the hero's downfall. Although fate may speed the action (for example, Edgar arrives at the prison just too late to save Cordelia in *King Lear* and Desdemona drops her handkerchief at the precise time and place most fatal for her in *Othello*), the prime cause of the hero's tragedy resides in some deficiency in his own character. This may be shown as an obsessive desire that blinds him to good or appropriate behaviour and will cause the death of others in addition to himself. Thus Othello is tormented by jealousy, and Macbeth made ruthless by ambition. The 'tragic flaw' may also be shown by an inability to do what is necessary, as in the case of the complex character Hamlet, whose procrastination springs from his deep melancholy.

The tragic hero is prey to some event that directly affects his deficiency, and the play reveals his consequent suffering and inner conflict. His stressful condition is contrasted with the noble, admirable life he led before, and from an early stage in the play we are given clues that he cannot escape a tragic end, for he is helplessly drawn along to his death by his own mistaken decisions.

There is no comprehensive scheme of reward and punishment in these tragedies, as is made clear by emphasising that the earlier praiseworthy career of the hero is a picture of him in 'normal' circumstances. Neither does tragedy come as a punishment for the evil the hero has committed during the course of the play, because such evil is not the hero's fault or 'true' wish. It comes as the result of the 'flaw' he can neither recognise nor overcome. His death is therefore deeply unsatisfactory to the audience, since it comes not as just punishment, but as the final blow in the tragedy. Minor characters too are swept up in the tragic whirl and die for no reason other than that they were in some sense contaminated by the hero. The play does not offer consolation, except in the sense of promising a new revitalised life for the survivors of the tragedy now that the death of the protagonist or protagonists marks the end of a dark era.

The feelings of an audience witnessing the tragic spectacle of a man's self-destruction in this way are complex. Aristotle, who first attempted an analysis of tragedy and its effects, considered that the spectator underwent 'catharsis', a purging of his emotions by suffering pity and terror during the play. Pity is provoked by seeing the torment of the hero and, possibly, the predicaments of minor characters entangled in his fate. Terror is aroused by the realisation that decisions and accidents out of the hero's control can cause the collapse of a kingdom as well as the death of a king.

These then are the essential ingredients of the four great Shakespearian tragedies. A good man of high birth and considerable influence is confronted with a problem, mystery or challenge. Uncharacteristically he is unable to deal with the situation because it tests an area of himself that is deficient. While he cannot solve the problem, neither can he turn away from it—it exerts a fascination upon him that amounts to an obsession. The play chronicles his steady, unrelenting path to ruin and death, and shows how his misguided actions cause the downfall of others and the collapse of society.

When we turn to look at the women in Shakespeare's plays we can see

clearly that the only two who might fulfil the requirements of this definition are Cleopatra and Juliet.

Anthony and Cleopatra is a curious and powerful play. Not only does it
have both a tragic hero paralleled by a heroine, but the extent to which
Cleopatra is truly 'tragic' in the sense outlined above is highly debat-
able.

The first condition is easily fulfilled. Cleopatra was monarch of 'great
Egypt' and we are constantly reminded both of her personal and her political power. Caesar himself, even after she has been seized by the
Roman soldiers who invade her monument and is in the humiliating
position of being presented as prize captive, says when she kneels to him:

> Arise! You shall not kneel:
> I pray you rise; rise, Egypt.
> (V.ii.113–14)

The words are not so much to impress us with Caesar's courtesy as to
make clear that Cleopatra is the Queen of Egypt and need kneel to no
man. Similarly, Charmian's last words remind us that Cleopatra's
death was

> fitting for a princess
> Descended of so many royal kings.
> (V.ii.325–6)

Both Charmian and Iras, her attendants, die with their mistress; Iras
from an envenomed kiss, and Charmian choosing rather to commit
suicide in the same way as Cleopatra than to live on without her. The
fates of these minor characters can perhaps therefore be seen as conditioned by the fate of the heroine.

Cleopatra is first shown to us in her court, provocative and teasing to
Anthony, already testing him to see where his loyalties and affections lie:

> You must not stay here longer; your dismission
> Is come from Caesar, therefore hear it, Anthony.
> Where's Fulvia's process? Caesar's would I say? Both?
> Call in the messengers. As I am Egypt's Queen
> Thou blushest Anthony, and that blood of thine
> Is Caesar's homager.
> (I.i.26–31)

The rapid taunting patter shows Cleopatra very much in control of the situation and of Anthony. He replies, anxious to deny any suggestion that he might be faithless, the seriousness and plainness of his speech a clear indication to the audience of his infatuation. Cleopatra's quick-witted jibes leave us uncertain as to her motives, an uncertainty height-ened by the fact that we are given no 'background' information about her customary moral excellence as we are about Anthony. Enobarbus and other Roman friends of Anthony comment darkly on his present weakness, contrasting it from the first moments of the play with the valour and good sense he possessed in the past:

> His captain's heart
> Which in the scuffles of great fights hath burst
> The buckles on his breast . . .
> . . . is become the bellows and the fan
> To cool a gypsy's lust.
> (I.i.6–10)

This forms part of the tragic pattern and points to Anthony's excessive susceptibility to Cleopatra's charms as his fatal flaw, but we have no parallel description of her. She is seen only in terms of the present, as a threat to Rome and Anthony. Enobarbus' attitude is clear; he calls her not only 'gypsy' but also 'strumpet'. Later it is true, we learn from an embittered Anthony that he found her 'as a morsel cold upon Dead Caesar's trencher,' and later still that she bore Caesar's child, Caes-arion, but this does not give the picture of a woman turned away from a good, moral life through the fault of having loved Anthony. Rather it suggests the opposite, that she was morally lax by nature, or, in terms of the tragedy, that she was the evil to Anthony's good, an Iago to Anthony's Othello.

For the earlier part of the play, Cleopatra's actions tend to support the view of her advanced by Anthony's friends. She is capable of violent, undignified bursts of temper (as in her attack on the Roman messenger). Her openness about her sexual relationships with Anthony shows a lack of reticence with her court attendants that suggests she is accustomed to many such affairs. (By comparison it is unthinkable, for example, that Desdemona would discuss Othello in a similar way.) Worst of all, Cleo-patra betrays Anthony by deserting him at the battle of Actium, causing him to call her 'this foul Egyptian!' and 'triple turn'd whore'. The accus-ation of political as well as sexual prostitution suggests that even Anthony sees promiscuity as her true nature. It is only when Cleopatra is confronted with the body of the dying Anthony that she attains the regal dignity that befits her position. Her tenderness and passion are unqualified by jokes or jibes beyond a pathetic attempt to rouse Anthony by accusing him of deserting her:

> Noblest of men, woo't die?
> Hast thou no care of me? Shall I abide
> In this dull world, which in thy absence is
> No better than a sty?
>
> (IV.xv.59–62)

But the attempt fails. Anthony is dead. The grandeur, passion and desolation of Cleopatra's next words make them some of the finest in the play:

> The crown o' th' earth doth melt. My lord!
> O, withered is the garland of the war,
> The soldier's pole is fallen: young boys and girls
> Are level now with men. The odds is gone,
> And there is nothing left remarkable
> Beneath the visiting moon.
>
> (IV.xv.63–8)

This sense of Cleopatra's dignity is sustained until her death. The harsh, feckless note has gone; she appears not only regal but courageous. Although it is the thought of being paraded in the streets of Rome that finally drives her to kill herself, the idea of suicide had been with her since Anthony's death:

> is it sin
> To rush into the secret house of death
> Ere death dare come to us?
>
> (IV.xv.80–2)

and again, to her attendants:

> Come; we have no friend
> But resolution, and the briefest end.
>
> (IV.xv.90–1)

The circumstances of her death fit the tragic pattern. It is the focal point of the final act, parallel in importance to that of Anthony, as indicated by Caesar's final speech in which he links their deaths in burial:

38

13 The figure of Cleopatra was romanticised in the eighteenth century, as reflected in the flamboyant costumes. Note the cascade of tulle from Miss Younge's headpiece, 1772

She shall be buried by her Anthony.
No grave upon the earth shall clip in it
A pair so famous. High events as these
Strike those that make them and their story is
No less in pity, than his glory which
Brought them to be lamented.

(V.ii.356–61)

At the end of the play we see Cleopatra honoured as a tragic heroine, but there does appear to be a marked difference in her character after the death of Anthony. There are two major questions still to be answered. First, did she have a fatal flaw that led her inexorably on to her own death, or was she merely the primary agent in Anthony's downfall, ultimately enmeshed by events outside her control? Second, is her character shown to deteriorate as a result of her deficiency? If it cannot be proved that she had a fatal weakness, revealed by a progressive worsening of her character during the play, then no matter how moving her death, she cannot properly be called a 'tragic heroine'.

If we return to the first three acts of the play we find some apparent inconsistencies within Cleopatra's character. Although she teases Anthony she is also respectful towards him, always addressing him as 'my lord' or 'Anthony', never qualified by the kind of vicious adjectives she employs for those she despises, 'scarce-bearded Caesar', for instance, or 'shrill-tongued Fulvia'. A similar note of respect, conveying the dignity of their passion, is expressed whenever Cleopatra speaks of Anthony or he of her. In the following passage, when Cleopatra is impatient for his return, she discusses Anthony with Charmian. Although there is an overtly sexual pun, which in another context would suggest frivolity, the tone and characteristic use of imagery to describe Anthony lend majesty both to the love and the lovers:

> Stands he, or sits he?
> Or does he walk? Or is he on his horse?
> O happy horse to bear the weight of Anthony!
> Do bravely, horse, for wot'st thou whom thou mov'st?
> The demi-Atlas of this earth, the arm and burgonet of men.
> (I.v.19–24)

Throughout the play our sense of their dignity remains constant no matter how shrill Cleopatra may be to the other characters nor how dulled Anthony's sense of responsibility becomes towards Rome. The very violence of Anthony's reaction after her fleet deserts him at Actium proves how deeply she has wounded him by this apparent betrayal:

> Betrayed I am.
> O this false soul of Egypt! This grave charm,
> Whose eye becked forth my wars and called them home,
> Whose bosom was my crownet, my chief end.
> (IV.xii.24–7)

40

Similarly, Cleopatra's need to test Anthony's love by her foolish prank of pretending to be dead reveals how much she depends on him. The strength of their passion for each other is equally balanced and it is therefore impossible to see Cleopatra as the evil instrument of Anthony's downfall. She is never shown to have any base motive for loving him, and the betrayal at Actium is a desertion of his military position, not of Anthony himself. Her devotion never wavers.

The quality of Cleopatra's feeling goes beyond the level of the animal sensuality recognised in her by the other characters in the play. Nowhere is the sublimity of her love shown more clearly than at the point of her death. Here her thoughts are already with Anthony, impatiently imagining that he awaits her:

> good Iras; quick: methinks I hear
> Anthony call: I see him rouse himself
> To praise my noble act . . .
> Husband, I come.
> (V.ii.282–4 and 286)

The intensity of Cleopatra's passion, her fidelity and queenly dignity cannot therefore be questioned. What still remains in doubt is whether this love can be called a tragic flaw, as it can for Anthony. Bearing in mind that the flaw and its consequences must come unexpectedly upon the hero or heroine because a new circumstance reveals it, the short answer is No. Cleopatra openly acknowledges her earlier lovers, and the pattern of their infatuation with her sounds very much like that of Anthony. Cleopatra is amusingly objective about it:

> Broad-fronted Caesar,
> When thou wast here above the ground, I was
> A morsel for a monarch; and great Pompey
> Would stand and make his eyes grow in my brow;
> There would he anchor his aspect, and die
> With looking on his life.
> (I.v.29–34)

Her love for Anthony is of a different kind. When Charmian teases her about Julius Caesar, Cleopatra says that their relationship existed in:

> My salad days,
> When I was green in judgement, cold in blood.
> (I.v.73–4)

41

14 Richard Johnson and Janet Suzman as Anthony and Cleopatra in 1972

Her present passion transcends all others, but there is no chronicling of her consequent downfall as there is for Anthony. He is shown as being increasingly under her influence, powerless to resist her, unable to make judgements. He ages and weakens in the course of the play, but nothing comparable is suggested for Cleopatra. We can see this most clearly in contrasting the reasons for their deaths. Anthony's comes as the culmination of a series of wrong decisions stemming from his increasing inability to give sound judgement. His love for Egypt's queen leads him to agree to fight Caesar by sea at Actium, and his subsequent defeat plunges him into humiliation, rage and despair. He falls for Cleopatra's trick, believing that she has killed herself out of remorse, but his own attempt at suicide fails. The pathos of his situation is intensely poignant:

at the last he has been so blinded and weakened by the defect in his character that he cannot even succeed in destroying himself. When he finally dies in Cleopatra's arms, there is no sense of triumph or justice—it is a ghastly error and the world is shaken by his loss.

> It were for me
> To throw my sceptre at the injurious gods,
> To tell them that this world did equal theirs
> Till they had stol'n our jewel. All's but naught.
> (IV.xv.75–8)

The unfolding of Cleopatra's character, on the other hand, is almost the reverse of Anthony's. What little information we are given about what she was like before the events of the play took place suggests that she was self-indulgent and, by Roman standards at least, brazenly promiscuous. The first three and a half acts of the play bear out these charges to a certain extent, but certainly do not show any *deterioration* in her character. On the contrary, we are made increasingly aware of her charismatic effect on all who encounter her:

> For her own person,
> It beggared all description: she did lie
> In her pavilion, cloth-of-gold, of tissue,
> O'er picturing that Venus where we see
> The fancy out-work nature.
> (Enobarbus, II.ii.197–201)

More significantly, as her end approaches she gains in nobility: unlike the wasteful catastrophe of Anthony's death, her death is a carefully calculated triumph over Caesar. Almost her last words, addressed to the fatal asp, are:

> O, couldst thou speak,
> That I might hear thee call great Caesar ass
> Unpolicied!
> (V.ii.306–8)

Although Caesar has conquered Egypt, she has defeated him by taking her life and depriving him of what would have been the climax of his victorious parade through the streets of Rome. Caesar confesses her triumph—'she levelled at[1] our purposes'—but his sense of having been cheated melts away when he looks at her. He is affected by her beauty,

---

[1] *levelled at*: both guessed and fought against.

even in death, and his usually cold and rational language gains a poetic dimension:

> she looks like sleep,
> As she would catch another Anthony
> In her strong toil of grace.
>
> (V.ii.344–6)

Her death contrasts with Anthony's, however, because we see it as the end of a noble, courageous and extraordinary woman, not as an event that shakes the fabric of society. Life in her court will change, but it will be because of Caesar's conquest, not Cleopatra's death. It is true that Iras and Charmian die with her, but theirs are in a sense *sympathetic* deaths—one on a kiss and the other a bravely chosen suicide. Her women are not helpless victims of Cleopatra's personal tragedy, unlike Anthony's soldiers who were decimated at Actium. Anthony and Cleopatra are linked by their passionate love for each other and their decisions to commit suicide. They are not linked by the effects of that love or the reasons for, and results of, their deaths. Cleopatra has no fatal flaw, and consequently there is no charting of a degeneration in her character as she approaches her end: indeed, there is no sense of the inevitability of her death, as there is of Anthony's. She cannot, therefore, be termed a true tragic heroine, although she comes closer to it than any other woman in Shakespeare.

From a less academic point of view, her personal tragedy is intensely convincing and moving. The poetic quality of the language in her death-scene rivals any to be found in *Othello*, *Macbeth*, *King Lear* or *Hamlet*. One of the main reasons *Anthony and Cleopatra* has proved so difficult to stage or film is not the technical problem of switching rapidly to and fro between Rome and Egypt, but the visual credibility of Cleopatra. By the magic of his poetry Shakespeare can conjure up the extraordinary fusion of opposites, the enigma, the luxurious sensuality; but it is hard to find an actress whose appearance and manner reflect these qualities. There is an elusive element in Cleopatra, and our prevailing vision of her at the close of the play is perhaps best summed up by Enobarbus:

> Age cannot wither her, nor custom stale
> Her infinite variety: other women cloy
> The appetite they feed, but she makes hungry
> Where most she satisfies.
>
> (II.ii.235–8)

Even death, cold proof of her mortality, is embraced with triumph:

> Show me, my women, like a queen: go fetch
> My best attires. I am again for Cydnus,
> To meet Mark Anthony . . .
> . . . Bring our crown and all.
>   (V.ii.226–8 and 231)

The whims, the paradoxes, the mystery and above all the supreme grandeur of Cleopatra, create a goddess-figure rather than a tragic heroine.

When we turn to consider Juliet, there is an immediate reduction in scale and change in tone. Here is no sensual goddess, but instead a young, innocent girl. The play is some twelve years earlier than *Anthony and Cleopatra*, written at a time when Shakespeare had not yet fully evolved the method he was to use for the great tragedies. Neither Romeo nor Juliet is shown to suffer any deficiency of character, for as the Prologue makes clear, they are the victims of circumstances beyond their control:

> Two households, both alike in dignity . . .
> From ancient grudge, break to new mutiny . . .
> From forth the fatal loins of these two foes,
> A pair of star-crossed lovers, take their life:
> Whose misadventur'd piteous overthrows,
> Doth with their death bury their parents' strife.

Romeo and Juliet were predestined to fall in love and kill themselves; 'fatal loins' suggests that their fate had been decided from the moment of conception. They are 'star-cross'd', so their destiny does not rest with any decision they may or may not take. The influences on them are *external*, so there is no inherent fault in either of their characters to explain their path to death. In consequence there is no evolution of character necessary to reveal the cancerous effects of a fatal flaw. The nobility and integrity of Romeo and Juliet remain unshaken throughout the course of the play. Similarly it would be redundant to tell us what they were like before tragedy overtook them because the audience is to be concerned with: 'The fearful passage of their death-marked love.' We are directed to follow the unfolding of the plot, not any subtle psychology of the characters themselves. It would therefore be nonsensical to apply

15 A rare sketch of the famous Irish actress, Eliza O'Neil, in her first appearance as Juliet in 1814

the same criteria that we used to test Cleopatra's claim as a tragic heroine. Juliet's stature can be measured only by comparing her with her lover, and what we need to establish is whether, given that they have no power over their own fates, Romeo and Juliet are of equal tragic significance in the play.

Romeo and Juliet is as much concerned with the theme of love as it is with the fates of its two young lovers. In many ways the two principal characters are puppets manipulated by fate, and they are made to act out a moral tale. Love is a teaching, healing force—we know from the Prologue that it is through the ill-starred love of their children that the Montagues and Capulets will be brought together: love triumphs over hate. The Prince of Verona voices the ironic moral:

> Capulet, Montague:
> See what a scourge is laid upon your hate!
> That heaven finds means to kill your joys with love!
> (V.iii.290–2)

Romeo and Juliet have been sacrificed so that peace and order can be restored, but they triumph in another way. Their love is unswervingly described as true and pure, an idealisation that could not withstand the test of time. Death cuts their love off when it is at its height and so it remains unspoilt—Romeo and Juliet triumph over time.

Throughout the course of their relationship, the lovers are described in parallel terms. The language they use is rapt, ecstatic and essentially chaste. Here Romeo notices Juliet dancing by and immediately falls in love:

> O she doth teach the torches to burn bright.
> It seems she hangs upon the cheek of night
> Like a rich jewel in an Ethiop's ear:
> Beauty too rich for use, for earth too dear. . . .
> Did my heart love till now, forswear it sight;
> For I ne'er saw true beauty till this night.
> (I.v.47–50 and 55–6)

Juliet too loves him on sight for she has barely learned his name when she declares to her nurse:

> My only love sprung from my only hate,
> Too early seen, unknown, and known too late,
> Prodigious birth of love it is to me
> That I must love a loathed enemy.
> (I.v.141–4)

No reason is suggested: it is fate, for she says that she *must* love him.

The purity of their love is emphasised throughout the play and the delicacy and dream-like quality of their speeches contrasts with the bawdy jokes of the servants. There is no hint of sexual banter between Romeo and Juliet as there is between Anthony and Cleopatra. Romeo can hardly bear to be parted from Juliet, yet he sees his desire for her as acceptable only within the conventional framework of a Christian marriage. He tells his confessor, Friar Laurence:

> my heart's dear love is set
> On the fair daughter of rich Capulet;
> As mine on hers, so hers is set on mine;
> And all combined, save what thou must combine
> By holy marriage.
>
> (II.iii.57–61)

The secret marriage takes place, but Romeo's banishment for killing Tybalt, Juliet's cousin, means that it may never be consummated. Juliet reacts characteristically:

> I'll to my wedding-bed
> And death, not Romeo, take my maidenhead!
> (III.ii.136–7)

Such a dire remedy is unnecessary, for Juliet's nurse and Friar Laurence arrange for Romeo to spend the night with Juliet. We do not see them together again until dawn heralds Romeo's final leave-taking. The idyllic quality of their now-consummated marriage is delicately conveyed by sustained pastoral imagery. Here Juliet implores Romeo to stay, desperately defying the reality of dawn:

> Wilt thou be gone? It is not yet near day:
> It was the nightingale, and not the lark,
> That pierc'd the fearful hollow of thine ear;
> Nightly she sings on yon pomegranate tree:
> Believe me, love, it was the nightingale.
> (III.v.1–5)

Never for a moment is there a faltering or questioning of their love for each other. In this focus on an impossible ideal, their feelings are also shown to be identical. It is the first time that either of them has fallen in love (his affair with Rosaline is superficial, for all thought of her goes when he finds Juliet); they are utterly faithful, and they prefer death to the thought of living without each other. Juliet therefore has equal status with Romeo. But is the play really a tragedy? We have already seen that through death their love triumphs over time and brings their families together, so the tragedy cannot lie there. It exists on a much more human level: two young lives are wasted, an experience of great beauty vanishes, and brave hopes are dashed to the ground. As proved by its

16 The delicate sexuality in *Romeo and Juliet* was given focus in this production with Anton Lesser and Judy Buxton, in 1980

enduring popularity, the play appeals both to the human desire for perfection and the harsh realisation that ideals cannot last:

> Never was a story of more woe
> Than this of Juliet and her Romeo.
>   (V.iii.308–9)

We are moved by Juliet's fate as we are by Romeo's; their tragedy affects us since it has a universal message. This is very different from what we feel at the end of *Anthony and Cleopatra*, where Cleopatra's death stuns us because of her personal stature. She is drawn as a far more complex and compelling character than Juliet.

Although their dramatic realisation and function are so different, Cleopatra and Juliet are the only women in Shakespeare who hold the centre of the stage in tragedy. Others are there for a brief moment, or else

17 These cartoon-like figures by Skelt from the late eighteenth century are arranged to suggest the contrast between the suave Venetian courtiers and the alien figure of Othello, insanely jealous and violent

play crucial supporting roles, and it is these we should now consider.

The pale saintly figure of Desdemona is a strange one. She must be one of the most mocked characters in Shakespeare, branded with virtually every derogatory term from two-dimensional and unreal to stupid. Most frequently she is seen as the pathetic victim of events far beyond her control, to die, as she says 'a guiltless death'. It is possible, however, to give a slightly different interpretation of her fate by assessing her behaviour in terms of Elizabethan social conventions for women.

Handbooks of the period explain in some detail what is required of the ideal wife, and Desdemona seems to fulfil even the most conservative expectation. She is beautiful but also humble:

> A maiden never bold
> Of spirit so still and quiet that her motion
> Blushed at herself.
>
> (I.iii.94–6)

Her concern for Cassio shows her generosity, for she will intercede for him with Othello. She is wise, and also a 'true and loving' wife—'the sweetest innocent that e'er did lift up eye'. However, there are other

50

aspects of her behaviour that would have caused an Elizabethan audience to look slightly askance at her.

An unmarried girl should never speak with a man unless an older woman is present. If negotiations for a marriage take place, they must be with the father's consent (and preferably in his presence), and be initiated by the young man. The girl's choice of husband—or rather, the choice made for her—must therefore rest on rational grounds and not personal choice.

Judged by these criteria, Desdemona falls down badly. She marries without consulting her father. Brabantio's first words on confronting Othello are: 'O thou foul thief, where hast thou stowed my daughter?' (I.ii.61). We then learn from Othello that she was so moved by the stories of his valour that:

> She gave me for my pains a world of sighs . . .
> And bade me, if I had a friend that loved her,
> I should but teach him how to tell my story,
> And that would woo her. Upon this hint I spake.'
> (I.iii.159 and 164–6)

So it was Desdemona who made the first move. She even boasts that it was love that drew her to him:

> That I love the Moor to live with him,
> My downright violence, and storm of fortunes
> May trumpet to the world.
> (I.iii.249–51)

Once married, she continues to commit slight offences against the correct code of conduct for the ideal wife. She is no sooner married than she leaves hearth and home (the traditional limits of the woman's realm) to be with Othello. She sees Cassio without her husband's permission and is far too concerned with Cassio's request. Her plan of how she will discuss the matter with Othello at every moment so that even 'his bed shall seem a school', shows far too much self-possession and strong will.

Desdemona has, therefore, some quite serious faults as a wife, including a will of her own, which was evident even before she was married. This does not mean that she merits the terrible accusations flung at her by Othello, nor does she in any way deserve her death, but she is partly responsible for the tragic action of the play. Othello's behaviour and mounting jealousy are made more comprehensible if we remember what Elizabethan husbands might expect of their wives.

There is a more fundamental problem with Desdemona and that is whether she is really credible as a character. It is certainly difficult to find her behaviour plausible, particularly in view of the fact that she can at times show a mind of her own. The first time we must seriously question her credibility is when Iago has led Othello to believe that she has slept with Cassio. Unwittingly, Desdemona brings up the subject of Cassio's reinstatement as an officer. They both misinterpret each other's words and finally Othello hits her, presumably in the face. Desdemona says meekly 'I have not deserved this', and when Othello tells her to go, does as he says, with 'I will not stay to offend you'. She suffers every subsequent insult and accusation without protest, beyond the constant reiteration of her innocence. She remains steadfastly humble and holy until her death, and even as he prepares to smother her she makes a pathetic plea to Othello: 'But while I say one prayer!' In his vengeful haste to destroy her, he refuses to listen which makes her last words keenly poignant. Emilia rushes in to the bedchamber before her mistress is dead; on hearing her voice she asks:

Emilia. O who hath done this deed?
Desd. Nobody. I myself. Farewell.
Commend me to my kind lord. O farewell!

In spite of the moving simplicity of her loyalty, a modern audience tends to find this unswerving devotion to God and Othello implausible. Dramatically, the effect of Desdemona's death is greater if we allow that she is not *intended* to mirror reality. There is certainly no development of her character during the course of the play and perhaps it is easiest to make sense of her by seeing her as a symbol of purity, her white against the black contaminating evil of Iago that sweeps over Othello.

Hamlet is not in any sense a black-and-white play. Few of the issues in it are clear, and critics argue incessantly over its meaning. It is also exceptional amongst the tragedies in having two important female roles: Ophelia and Gertrude. Unlike Desdemona, Ophelia is not guilty of showing a dangerously strong mind of her own. Indeed, much of Ophelia's personal tragedy is that she has insufficient strength to sustain her after Hamlet's inexplicably harsh treatment and her father's murder. She is driven insane with grief, and Gertrude relates how she has fallen into a stream:

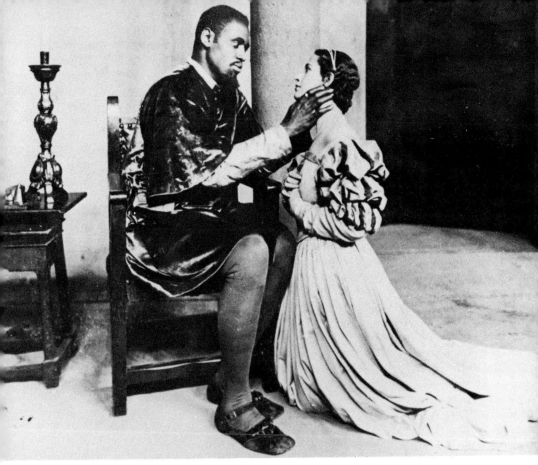

18 Paul Robeson and Peggy Ashcroft in the renowned production of *Othello* in 1930

> Her clothes spread wide,
> And mermaid-like awhile they bore her up. . . .
> But long it could not be
> Till that her garments, heavy with their drink,
> Pulled the poor wretch from her melodious lay
> To muddy death.
>
> (IV.vii.174–5 and 179–82)

The pathos of her drowning—still singing, she is drawn down under the water—is mirrored in the delicate harmonies of this speech. Gertrude's vision of her death presents her to us as a poor innocent, oblivious of danger to the last.

But another aspect of Ophelia is traced in her characterisation. Like Desdemona she has originally gone against social mores by seeing a young man unchaperoned and without her father's approval. Polonius is not as violently opposed to Hamlet as Brabantio is to Othello, but he tells Ophelia that he has heard she has been seeing Hamlet alone, and wants to know exactly what is going on. When she answers 'he hath importuned me with love In honourable fashion', he pours scorn on her naïvety and insists that Hamlet only wants her sexual favours. Laertes, her brother, has said the same and warned her not to lay her 'chaste treasure open To his unmastered opportunity'. From the outset, therefore, the seed is planted in the audience's mind not only that Hamlet presents some kind of threat to Ophelia, but that, unwittingly, she is encouraging him.

After the stringent warnings from her father and brother, Ophelia meekly agrees to spurn any further advances that Hamlet may make. We do not see her on stage with him until Act III (his relationship with Ophelia is, after all, subsidiary to the main preoccupation of the play: how to avenge his father's murder). In the meantime Ophelia tells Polonius she has been 'affrighted' by Hamlet, pale and distraught, suddenly coming into her private room. He does not speak to her, but holds her by the wrist and stares at her; even when he leaves he is unable to take his eyes off her, 'And to the last bended their light on me'. Both she and Polonius interpret his behaviour as arising from 'the very ecstasy of love', but there is no indication from Hamlet that this is so. When they meet in Act III Hamlet asks her cruelly ambiguous questions about her chastity. Ophelia is unable to understand what he means and her utter inability to spar wittily with him leads Hamlet on to taunt her more and more. It is almost as if he is desperately trying to get some spark of reaction from her. He cuts as deeply as he can, insulting her adored father, accusing her of promiscuity, rejecting her harshly:

> Get thee
> To a nunnery. Go, farewell. Or if thou
> Wilt needs marry, marry a fool, for wise men know well
> Enough what monsters you make of them.
>
> (III.i.139–42)

After he has gone out, Ophelia speaks of herself as 'of ladies most deject and wretched' for having once been moved by his 'musicked vows', which mean nothing now that his 'noble mind is here o'er thrown'.

But Hamlet has not yet finished with her. At the play that he has arranged to prick Claudius' conscience, he chooses to sit with Ophelia as 'metal more attractive' than his mother. Hamlet cracks bawdy jokes to humiliate Ophelia and at first she shows a total innocence of his meaning:

Hamlet. Lady, shall I lie in your lap?
Ophelia. Ay, my lord.
Ham. I mean my head upon your lap?
Oph. Ay, my lord.
Ham. Do you think I mean country[2] matters?
Oph. I think nothing, my lord.
Ham. That's a fair thought to lie between maids' legs.
Oph. What is, my lord?
Ham. · Nothing.

(III.ii.110–19)

Ophelia's naïvety must be assumed and not genuine, because later she gives as good as she gets:

Ophelia. You are keen[3] my lord, you are keen.
Hamlet. It would cost you a groaning to take off mine edge.
Oph. Still better, and worse.

(III.ii.248–50)

Hamlet immediately changes the subject, almost as if embarrassed. He has only been playing with Ophelia, boosting his own confidence by superior joking sneers at her innocence. The hint that she might be quite happy to indulge in verbal flirtation brings Hamlet up short and reminds him of his true purpose: to expose Claudius' treachery. Ophelia makes no further significant contribution to this scene. The fact that the precise nature of her relationship with Hamlet has been called in question from the first, together with her disingenuous puns, gives an aura of suppressed sexuality to their relationship. In view of this, the tenor of her speeches once she had gone mad is not so uncharacteristic as is often supposed. As she herself says: 'we know what we are, but Know not what we may be' (IV.v.41–2).

Ophelia is initially shown as having a close, affectionate relationship with three men: her brother, her father and Hamlet. Laertes goes back to university in Paris early in the play and does not return to Denmark until too late to be of any assistance or counsel to Ophelia. Polonius, with the best of motives, interferes with Hamlet and Ophelia's relationship, but is killed before the tensions he has done much to help create have any chance of being resolved. Ophelia's only prop after Act III is thus Hamlet, the man whose behaviour she now finds incomprehensible,

---

[2] *country*: The sexual pun on this word was frequently made in Elizabethan writing, but is not always recognised today. Were it not spelt with an 'o', the other meaning would be immediately recognisable.
[3] *keen*: clever, and also sexually aroused.

who insults and mocks her, and who, above all, has murdered her father. Then, even he is sent away, so effectively Ophelia is left alone to endure her grief. Sorrow overwhelms her and she is distracted with thinking obsessively of her dead father:

> I cannot choose but weep to think they would
> lay him i' th' cold ground.
>
> (IV.v.68–9)

The lyrical poetry of her songs is moving and its delicacy befits her feeling for the father whose death she so mourns, but there are other elements in her now crazed speech. She turns suddenly to bawdy ballads:

> Young men will do't if they come to't,
> By Cock[4] they are to blame.
> Quoth she, 'Before you tumbled me
> You promised me to wed.'
> He answers:
> 'So would I 'a' done, by yonder sun,
> An thou hadst not come to my bed.'
>
> (IV.v.59–65)

Now that Ophelia is 'divided from herself and her fair judgement' she does not trouble to hide any crude thoughts that may flit through her mind. This does not mean that she is not chaste. On the contrary, Shakespeare is surely showing us through Ophelia's madness that the girl most conscious of chastity is the one who is most distracted by sexual imaginings. Ophelia's 'ravings' relate directly to the two essentials of her personality: her deep love for her father and her worry about the nature of her relationship with Hamlet.

Ophelia's main function in the play is to illuminate a particular facet of Hamlet's decline. She has known him both in friendship and gallant devotion and so is especially fitted to utter the famous speech beginning: 'O what a noble mind is here o'er thrown!' In addition, her death gives an added spur to Laertes' revenge against Hamlet, and her burial brings them suddenly face to face as they leap into her grave to fight out the proof of their affection for her.

Since her relationship with Hamlet is subsidiary to the main interest of the play, Ophelia's dramatic significance is frequently reduced to a structural one. It is true that she never challenges the wishes of father,

[4] *cock*: God, but also slang for penis, as in Modern English.

" His beard as white as snow,
All flaxen was his poll ;
He is gone, he is gone,
And we cast away moan :
God ha' mercy on his soul !"

19 A startling portrayal by Lily Brayton in 1905 of Ophelia's madness after Hamlet has rejected her

brother or Hamlet and is borne along by the plot much as the cold stream takes her to her death, but it is also true that Shakespeare gives her briefly-sketched personality sufficient dimension to make her psychologically credible. Her youthful chastity and anguished heart are implicitly contrasted with the venery and insensitivity of Hamlet's mother, Gertrude.

It is evident from the first that there is much more to Claudius' marriage to Gertrude than he wishes Hamlet and the court to know. He is far too rational, insisting on the propriety of the marriage by claiming that its joy can thus outweigh the sorrow of his brother-in-law's death. It is all too smooth, too perfectly balanced to convey sincerity:

> now our Queen, . . .
> Have we, as 'twere, with a defeated joy,
> With an auspicious and a dropping eye.
> With mirth in funeral, and with dirge in marriage,
> In equal scale weighing delight and dole,
> Taken to wife.
> (I.ii.8–14)

Gertrude evinces no such need to justify her actions and thereby does not betray any sense of guilt. She is concerned with her present good fortune, and neither lingers over the death of her first husband nor analyses her motives in taking another. Her unfeeling haste in marrying Claudius cuts Hamlet to the heart. He condemns his mother for her fickleness that within

> A little month, or ere those shoes were old
> With which she followed my poor father's body
>   (I.ii.147–8)

she was the wife of his hated uncle. Gertrude is therefore immensely important to the play, because Hamlet cannot accept her 'infidelity' to his father. Ophelia becomes obsessively concerned with her father's death because of the love she bore him in life, but her madness is only a pale reflection of Hamlet's devotion to his mother.

Gertrude is wholly ignorant of Claudius' successful plot against her first husband and equally oblivious of Hamlet's protectively possessive feelings towards her. She finds his melancholic behaviour exasperating, and is unable to understand why he will not rejoice with the rest of the court at her marriage. She seems a kindly, slow-witted, rather self-indulgent woman, in no way the emotional or intellectual equal of her son. When Hamlet finally determines to make her see the ghastly error of her choice his cruelly-chosen words force her to feel guilty:

> O Hamlet, speak no more.
> Thou turn'st mine eyes into my very soul,
> And there I see such black and grained spots
> As will not leave their tinct.
>   (III.iv.88–91)

Hamlet's appeal is not to her reason, or even to her finer feelings, but rather he forces her to view Claudius with intense sexual revulsion. He accuses her of marrying him only:

>   to live
> Stewed in corruption, honeying and making love
> Over the nasty sty . . .
>   (III.iv.91–3)

Gertrude is so sickened that she interrupts her son, begging him to stop for: 'These words like daggers enter in my ears.' She offers no explanation of her desire to marry Claudius, and so we must assume that the reason she cannot bear Hamlet's words is that they are true. He begs her not to sleep with Claudius again, but although she promises not to tell anyone what he has said, she avoids giving a direct answer. It may be that Gertrude is attempting a practical compromise: she wants to calm Hamlet but cannot bring herself to swear to something she will not be able to do. No clue as to her subsequent sexual relationship with Claudius is given, and it is up to the producer of the play to decide whether to leave the situation as ambiguous as it is when read, or to introduce some element in the acting to show that Gertrude definitely decided one way or the other.

Certainly she is fond of Hamlet. Not only is she prepared to listen to him when he storms at her, proof that he is sufficiently close to her to have a right to make comments on her personal life, but she is unfailingly concerned about him. A telling moment is when Hamlet comes forward at Ophelia's burial and grapples with Laertes. Claudius gives the cold command: 'Pluck them asunder,' but Gertrude calls out her son's name and begs the King to be patient with him. Her approach is direct and springs from a true maternal instinct. When she has drunk from the poisoned cup, almost her last words are: 'O my dear Hamlet!' The simple endearment is very poignant, reminding us that the bond between mother and son, and Hamlet's desperate jealousy of Claudius, account for as much of the tragic progress of the play as the need to avenge old Hamlet's death.

Desdemona, Ophelia and Gertrude all die because of direct association with the fate of a tragic hero, but none of their deaths approaches the wanton destruction of tender innocence witnessed in *King Lear*.

Lear is very old—'fourscore and upward'—and has arranged for the division of his kingdom between his three daughters in order that he may abdicate and live out his last years with Cordelia, the youngest:

I lov'd her most, and thought to set my rest
On her kind nursery.
(I.i.122–3)

Her elder sisters, Goneril and Regan, are already married, and so the land apportioned to Cordelia will be her dowry. The divisions have been made, but Lear wants to satisfy a strange whim before he will make a

20 The Gertrude in this 1850 production conveys emotion only by her anguished gaze in the closet scene. Her physical composure (reflected in the relaxed hands and carefully adjusted crown) would seem unrealistic to a twentieth-century audience. Hamlet was played by Mr Phelps and Gertrude by Miss Glyn

public proclamation. Perhaps it is a last autocratic gesture or even a need for reassurance now that he is dropping the reins of power which leads him to demand of his daughters:

> Which of you shall we say doth love us most,
> That we our largest bounty may extend
> Where nature doth with merit challenge.[5]
> (I.i.51–3)

He is well pleased with the effusive speeches of Goneril and Regan, whose ridiculous exaggerations make it clear that their words are false, stemming from greed and not love. When it comes to her turn, Cordelia can say nothing. Lear is enraged and humiliated. It is clear that he expects her protestation of love to exceed that of her sisters, partly because he must sense that it is genuinely so, but largely because she is his favourite. He hints as much in a gently jocular fashion when he first puts the question to her:

> Now, our joy,
> Although the last, not least . . .
> . . . What can you say to draw
> A third more opulent than your sisters? Speak.
> (I.i.82–3 and 85–6)

His terrible wrath when she fails him is so violent because her reticence is totally unexpected and has made him look a fool. In wounded, angry pride he refuses to listen to Kent's intercession on her behalf and gives her third of the inheritance to Goneril and Regan. Kent is banished for his pains, and Cordelia, now without a dowry, is rejected by the Duke of Burgundy, earlier an ardent suitor. The King of France, however, recognises that 'she is herself a dowry' and takes her off to be his wife. Lear dismisses her cruelly:

> we
> Have no such daughter nor shall ever see
> That face of hers again. Therefore be gone,
> Without our grace, our love, our benison.
> (I.i.262–5)

The moment that Lear had evidently planned as the glorious prelude to his abdication (public protestations of filial love from his daughters, fol-

---

[5] *where nature . . . challenge*: i.e., if filial love exceeds legal entitlement.

61

lowed by a show of his generosity in dividing up his kingdom for them), has gone irretrievably awry. He has banished Kent, an old and trusted counsellor, and been forced by her silence to send away the daughter he loved most. Such 'hideous rashness' must result in tragedy and there is a sombre indication of it at the end of the scene in which Goneril and Regan agree to stand together against him if need be.

Why cannot Cordelia speak? It is obvious that she does love him, but something prevents her from actually voicing her feelings:

> my love's
> More ponderous than my tongue,
> (I.i.77–8)

she says, and again:

> Unhappy that I am, I cannot heave
> My heart into my mouth.
> (I.i.91–2)

Her father tries to force her, but she can state in simple, unemotional language, only that she obeys, loves and honours him as duty requires. It is not the avowal that Lear wants, and he finds her unvarnished words harsh and ungrateful. This failure to comprehend her true meaning because personal vanity has so distorted his vision, is at the heart of Lear's tragedy. Cordelia's own is that he has asked her for the one thing she cannot give, and the whole plot of the play springs from her failure to live up to his expectations.

Generations of readers have been vexed by the problem presented by Cordelia's reticence. Although her integrity and genuine feeling are never questioned, no reason is advanced by herself or the other characters as to *why* she finds herself unable to take part in the game of declarations that Lear has masterminded. Ironically, the answer may lie in the words Goneril uses to describe her own affection:

> Sir, I love you more than word can wield the matter ...
> A love that makes breath[6] poor, and speech unable.
> (I.i.55 and 60)

For Cordelia this was only too painfully true. Her very silence is proof enough to the audience of her love, and contrasts with the outpourings of

---

[6] *breath*: language.

her sisters. She recognises her lack of 'that glib and oily art To speak and purpose not', and is glad not to have it even though it has cost her her father's favour.

Cordelia's sensitivity and high-minded resolution make such a powerful impression on us that it comes as a surprise to realise that she is absent from the play for long periods of time and speaks in all barely a hundred lines. Giving us such little sight of her on stage helps both to sustain her credibility and add to her mystery. Other characters mention her, and the picture they give is consistent with what we see on stage. When Kent asks how she received the letter which brought news of Lear's treatment at the hands of Goneril and Regan, we learn that she wept and:

> once or twice she heav'd the name of 'father'
> Pantingly forth, as if it press'd her heart;
> Cried 'Sisters! Sisters! Shame of ladies! Sisters!
> Kent! Father! Sisters! What i' th' storm? i' th' night?
> Let pity not be believed!' There she shook
> The holy water from her heavenly eyes.
>   (IV.iii.26–31)

Strong feelings make her inarticulate; the thought of her father's suffering causes her such sympathetic agony that she can hardly utter his name.

At the last, when she and Lear have been taken prisoner, her care is only for him. Her father tries to comfort and reassure her with a crazed vision of their future life together in prison. The simple delights and resolution of their present difficulties which he confidently expects are so hopelessly out of keeping with the harsh reality of what Edmund intends as to be most painful:

> We two alone will sing like birds i' the cage:
> When thou dost ask me blessing I'll kneel down
> And ask of thee forgiveness: so we'll live,
> And pray, and sing and tell old tales, and laugh
> At gilded butterflies.[7]
>   (V.iii.9–13)

Cordelia, not insane and only too aware of her father's failing mind and the cruel truth of his likely fate, cannot answer him. Our last sight of the two of them before her death shows Lear still babbling and blustering;

[7] *gilded butterflies*: exotically dressed courtiers.

21 After two hundred years of a sentimental version, Macready's production of *King Lear* restored Shakespeare's text in 1835. The refusal to allow a 'happy ending' for Lear and Cordelia and Edgar distressed and appalled many members of the audience. Cordelia was played by Helen Faucit

Cordelia, silent, weeping. Because of her unvarying tenderness towards her father, thereby adding warmth to her upright moral nature, Cordelia's death comes as a savage blow. It is the more terrible because it was almost prevented: she was hanged in prison as the result of Edmund's order, countermanded too late, to make it appear that she took her own life. One of the most moving stage directions in Shakespeare must be: *Re-enter Lear, with Cordelia dead in his arms.*

In terms of her function, Cordelia's relationship with Lear is central to the progress of the play. She also acts as a sounding-board by which the audience can assess the honesty or dishonesty of the other characters. The plain-spoken few (such as Kent, Edgar and the King of France) are allied with her, while the sly (notably Goneril, Regan and Edmund) are revealed by their hypocrisy and contrasted with her straightforwardness. It is possible to view her purely in symbolic terms, dramatising the notion that plainness is more honest and valuable than flattery or even eloquence.

Her position is therefore both structurally and thematically crucial, although she plays a passive part in the actual development of the plot.

To turn to Lady Macbeth after Cordelia is to turn from the innocent lamb to the ravenous wolf. Her hungry ambition for her husband to be king over-rides all other desires and responsibilities. When she learns of the witches' prophecy that Macbeth will ultimately be monarch, she fears he will be too kind-hearted to speed the day by murdering Duncan and determines to steel him to it herself. Her soliloquy imploring dark powers to take all compassion from her is appalling in its unnaturalness:

> Come, you spirits
> That tend on mortal[8] thoughts, unsex me here,
> And fill me, from the crown to the toe, top-full
> Of direst cruelty!
>
> (I.v.40–3)

She emerges as a negation of good, boldly defying heaven:

> Come, thick night,
> And pall thee in the dunnest smoke of hell
> That my keen knife see not the wound it makes,
> Nor heaven peep through the blanket of the dark,
> To cry 'Hold! Hold!'
>
> (I.v.50–4).

[8] *mortal*: concerned with death.

The imagery of blood, violence, darkness and death reflects her true nature, for from the first she is set on an unrelenting course of destruction. This is not to say that her lust for power is a fatal flaw—we are given no hint that before the events of the play she was a good woman, now perverted. Neither does her character decline, for her final, fatal madness comes suddenly.

There is a fundamental difference between Lady Macbeth and Macbeth, for he is introduced as the admirable and 'brave Macbeth—well he deserves that name'. It is only when 'vaulting ambition', unleashed by his wife's provocation, so seeps into his proper nature that he can admit:

> I am in blood
> Stepped in so far that should I wade no more,
> Returning were as tedious as go o'er.
> (III.iv.136–8)

The looming gargantuan figure of his wife is shown as consistently evil. Her function is to give Macbeth the vital initial push and then sustain him until he can hold his own against his conscience. Once this has been achieved, she ceases to take an active part in the play.

The unfailing technique that Lady Macbeth uses to keep Macbeth to his purpose is to taunt him with suggestions of effeminacy and cowardice. As she herself possesses characteristics that are traditionally held to be possible only in the male—single-minded courage and cruelty—she can twit Macbeth for his failure to live up to the standard that she, a mere woman, has set. The combination of tender woman's body and savage man's mind is clearly shown when Lady Macbeth derides her husband for being unable to face the murder of Duncan, now that time and place are right:

> I have given suck, and know
> How tender 'tis to love the babe that milks me;
> I would, while it was smiling in my face,
> Have plucked my nipple from his boneless gums,
> And dashed the brains out, had I so sworn as you
> Have done to this.
> (I.vii.54–9)

Nothing daunts her, and her courage has a practical side too. It is she who works out the details of the plan to kill the king, and when Macbeth is too frightened to return the blood-stained daggers to

22 The disquieting similarity between Mrs Charles Kean as Lady Macbeth and Queen
Victoria is a curious tribute to the Queen's effect on women's fashions, even for the stage

Duncan's room, she immediately takes command of the situation, sweeping him aside with:

> Infirm of purpose!
> Give me the daggers.
>   (II.ii.51–2)

She organises and covers up for Macbeth, whether it is to insist they wash their blood-stained hands after the murder of Duncan, or to give a plausible explanation to the guests of Macbeth's strange behaviour at his feast. Macbeth is so unsettled by seeing the ghost of Banquo at the table that he almost exposes their guilt. Lady Macbeth tries her old trick of ridicule—'Are you a man?'—but it does not silence him. She explains to the guests that he is subject to fits, but when Macbeth's gibbering about the spectre leads his guests to start asking questions, she quickly ends the feast and sends them home. In support of her husband for the furthering of his political designs, she is thus shown to be infinitely devious and resourceful.

Up to and including the feast-scene, Lady Macbeth appears to be ruthlessly strong, her conscience untroubled by the ghastly murder to which she was party or by the knowledge of her husband's subsequent crimes. From this point on, Macbeth assumes her dark, bloodied mantle of unrelenting ambition. He is able to contemplate the murders of Macduff, his wife, children and any other descendants as if it were a business matter. Lady Macbeth's function is therefore at an end by Act IV, and she now disappears from the play until the famous sleep-walking scene in Act V. Her gentlewoman informs us that she has gone mad. When Lady Macbeth appears the cause is obvious, for the realisation of her guilt has demented her, and she obsessively recalls the murder of Duncan:

> Here's the smell of the blood still. All the perfumes of Arabia will not sweeten this little hand.
>
>   (V.i.48–9)

We do not see her again after this scene. Her madness is one aspect of the general collapse and chaos that attend the final convulsive throes of the tragedy, but her death is insignificant in itself. It happens off-stage and we are given no information as to method or circumstance. Macbeth dismisses it as a mere inconvenience:

23 Ellen Terry as Lady Macbeth in the sleep-walking scene, 1888

Seyton. The Queen, my lord, is dead.
Macbeth. She should have died hereafter.
                    (V.v.16–17)

Her insanity and consequent death have no bearing on the course of the tragedy and she is in no sense a tragic heroine. Because her nature is of such unmitigated evil, neither are we able to feel sympathy for her on a personal level. Her crimes are so enormous that her only hope lies in God's forgiveness. As her doctor says, she is beyond help on this earth: 'more needs she the divine than the physician'. Any pathos that might be evoked by her sleep-walking scene is cancelled out by constant reminders of her horrendous brutality. She remains Shakespeare's most terrifying female figure.

Lady Macbeth's claim to this dubious honour rests not only on the grim catalogue of her crimes, but also on the credibility of her character. We cannot be deeply disturbed by a creation that is patently unreal, and this is why Tamora, the vengeful Queen of the Goths in *Titus Andronicus* cannot seriously disquieten us, even though she is far more blood-thirsty than Lady Macbeth.

Titus Andronicus is a murder-mystery, a thriller in which characterisation is neglected in favour of action. There are multiple plots and multiple atrocities; the audience's sensibilities are assaulted by horror after horror, each more gruesome and bizarre than the last.

Since it is one of the least frequently read or performed of Shakespeare's plays, a brief plot-summary is justified so that we may see Tamora's case in perspective.

The Roman General, Titus Andronicus, returns in triumph to Rome, bringing the Queen Tamora, her three sons and various other Goths as captives. In spite of Tamora's pleading, Titus hands her eldest son over to his own four sons so that they may hack him to pieces and burn the remains to compensate them for atrocities suffered by the Romans in battle. Later the Emperor chooses Tamora as his bride and she uses her position to plot against Titus. Lavinia, Titus' daughter, and her friend Bassianus, discover Tamora in a compromising situation with a lover. Frightened that they will report her to the Emperor, Tamora allows her two sons to rape Lavinia, ensuring her silence by tearing out her tongue and cutting off her hands. Bassianus is murdered. After more murder because of misdirected justice, Lavinia finally conveys the truth to

Titus. He pretends to be mad and tricks Tamora into leaving her guilty sons at his house. Titus cuts their throats, Lavinia catches the blood in a basin and they are served up in a pie to Tamora at a feast. The play ends with virtually everyone stabbing everyone else, although Titus' eldest son survives the holocaust to become the next Emperor.

Tamora's revenge on Titus is 'justified' in the sense that her sons' rape and mutilation of Lavinia cancels out Titus' sons butchering of her eldest boy, but such Mafia-like tidying up of wrongs hardly constitutes characterisation. Tamora is inhuman, a cardboard cut-out, who could well be the personification of Revenge that she does indeed adopt in Act V:

> I am Revenge; sent from the infernal kingdom
> To ease the gnawing vulture of thy mind
> By working wreakful vengeance on thy foes.
> (V.ii.30–2)

She is so wooden, so lacking in human compassion, self-doubt and guilt, that we cannot be truly moved, even by her heartless treatment of Lavinia.

Lavinia too is presented without subtlety, which is possibly fortunate, because her fate would otherwise be impossible for an audience to bear. As it is, her appearance on stage, raped and bleeding, is almost as horrific a moment as the putting out of Gloucester's eyes in *King Lear*. As if physical brutality were not enough, Tamora's sons leer cruel jokes in their victim's face:

Demetrius.	So, now go tell, and if thy tongue can speak, Who 'twas that cut thy tongue and ravished thee.
Chiron.	Write down thy mind, bewray thy meaning so, And if thy stumps will let thee play the scribe.
Dem.	See, how with signs and tokens she can scrowl.[9]
Chi.	Go home, call for sweet water, wash thy hands.
Dem.	She hath no tongue to call, nor hands to wash; And so let's leave her to her silent walks.
Chi.	An 'twere my case I should go hang myself.
Dem.	If thou hadst hands to help thee knit the cord.
	(II.iv.1–10)

It is repugnant to read and very unusual in Shakespeare, for there is no trace of humanity in these characters. Their words are such an odious

---

[9] *scrowl*: scrawl.

71

mixture of vicious sexuality and gratuitous violence as to approach pornography. Such writing was fashionable in Shakespeare's day, but we may be thankful that he rapidly lost interest in it.

Lavinia suffers as the direct result of Demetrius' and Chiron's attack, but indirectly and ultimately because her pain would cause her father to suffer. Other innocent bystanders who became casualties in the tragedies include Emilia, Iago's wife, and Lady Macduff. These minor characters are interesting because they exemplify the notion that tragedy of its nature (whether caused by a fatal flaw or by the external operation of fate), takes many victims in addition to the main protagonists. They also show that on every level of life in these plays, tragedy can provoke cruel and arbitrary judgements: integrity and loyalty are not proof against a violent death. Even if evil is punished, good is not necessarily rewarded.

Emilia is unremarkable as a character, apart from her unswerving loyalty to Desdemona and her insistence on plain speaking. Ironically these very virtues cause her downfall, for when she exposes her husband's treachery, he stabs her.

Lady Macduff is even further removed from the centre of tragedy in *Macbeth*. Fearing the witches' prophecy that Macduff may take his crown, Macbeth plans to murder the whole family and sends hired killers to their castle. A messenger begs Lady Macduff to leave with her children. Her reply—'Whither should I fly? I have done no harm'—jolts us with its naïve assumption that therefore she will be safe. Within moments her child is killed before her eyes and she is chased out crying 'Murder!' Shakespeare's tragedies are a terrifying mirror of life in their reiterated declaration that no one, high or low, young or old, can be guaranteed immunity from a cruel end.

Some of the minor women characters chose to die out of loyalty to their mistresses. We have seen that this was the case with Iras and Charmian, Cleopatra's attendants. On finding Juliet apparently dead, her nurse exclaims:

O me, O me! My child, my only life,
Revive, look up; or I will die with thee!
(IV.v.19–20)

and as she lies dying, Emilia begs Othello: 'O, lay me by my mistress' side.' Such protestations go beyond the bounds of the convention that a

24 The relationship between Juliet and her nurse (here played by Ellen Terry and Fanny Stirling in 1882) is a close and affectionate one

good servant is loyal to her mistress. They are there to heighten our sense of tragedy by reminding us that the heroine was held as uniquely precious even by those as lowly as her servants.

Although none of the women in Shakespeare attains the tragic stature of the great heroes like Hamlet and Lear, they are far more than mere props for the main structure of the plays. Linked by their unmerited deaths, their personalities span a subtle but wide range from Cleopatra, who wields considerable power in her own right, to Cordelia, who is unable to control any party of her destiny. With the exception of the women in *Titus Andronicus*, each of these characters is memorable because of her stamp of individuality, no matter how lightly Shakespeare may have imprinted it.

III

Women in the Comedies and Last Plays

> Come, come, we are friends: let's have a
> dance ere we are married.
>
> *Much Ado About Nothing* V.iv. 116–17

If the dark realm of Shakespeare's tragedies is essentially men's territory, pride of place in the bright panorama of his comedies must surely belong to the women. Set alongside vivacious heroines like Rosalind, Beatrice or Viola, their male counterparts pale into insignificance. The character of Beatrice, indeed, has such force and charm that interest in her eventually takes over the play, despite the fact that her fate is not an important aspect of the original plot.

Why should the women leap into prominence? One reason may be that Shakespeare found their traditional attributes of modesty, intuition and high-spiritedness highly suitable material for his comedies, and in varying blends and degrees, all his comic heroines have these characteristics. They never go beyond the bounds of what an Elizabethan audience would have found acceptable in a woman: it is rather that Shakespeare exalts the positive, rather than the negative traits. Any women that go against prevailing conventions are redeemed by the end of the play. Thus Katharina in *The Taming of the Shrew* is forced to give in to Petruchio's will, and Helena's unfeminine pursuit of Bertram is justified by the fact that he had failed to recognise her true worth; once he does so, she is submissive.

Another reason is that Shakespeare tacitly accepts the medieval idea of a hierarchy of nature in which woman is second to man. This means that the high seriousness of tragedy, with its intense focus on the fate of the individual, is an unsatisfactory setting for all but a very few women, and even these have their destinies inescapably intertwined with those of the tragic heroes. Comedy, on the other hand, allows for a broader, more detached view of society and a lighter tone. Although moral issues

75

are not excluded (*The Merchant of Venice* is very much concerned with the contrast between material and spiritual wealth, as well as the nature of justice), we do not become anxious or painfully involved with the characters and, as the play progresses, hints are given that everything will turn out all right in the end. The characters themselves are frequently capricious, willing to compromise, and although they may well have faults, these do not inspire *fear* in the audience, as would be the case in tragedy. The plots too are full of twists and turns, surprises and coincidences. Until the final scene makes everything clear, no decision is incapable of being changed or reversed.

The forces of charm and whimsy are so strong in his comedies as to offer a further strong indication as to why Shakespeare favoured women-characters for the leading roles. His choice was not a foregone conclusion, for other Elizabethan writers of comedy—notably Ben Jonson—let men dominate the stage as in tragedy. In the sixteenth century there were two traditions of dramatic comedy. One was the satirical revelation of human errors, played out so that the audience laughed to see their own follies so skilfully exposed. The other was to use as a setting some upset, sadness or problem that is subsequently resolved happily. Jonson wrote in the first, more hard-hitting tradition, where we laugh *at* the characters; Shakespeare in the second where we laugh *with* them. The hallmark of Shakespeare's comedies is consequently the move towards reconciliation and a restoration of order by the correct understanding of the original problem. Unlike the tragedies, which insist that chaos can be averted only by the elimination of those swept up in the catastrophe, the comedies show that problems can be solved and sorrows overcome if the situation is properly understood by those involved in it. Although we laugh at comedy, its purpose is as realistic and serious as that of tragedy: comedy shows us that happiness results from being able to face problems and put them into a balanced perspective; tragedy shows that misery and death result when dilemmas loom so large as to blot out all other aspects of life. As with the tragedies it is impossible to impose a strict formula on the construction of the comedies beyond the pattern mentioned above: that they all begin with the characters perplexed or threatened, but end happily. This general definition serves to embrace the eleven usually termed 'comedies' by editors and the five 'last plays'.

The agents of happiness and order in Shakespeare's comedies are the heroines, and their function is therefore of supreme importance. Not only do the women have the leading roles but also they are more numerous than in the other types of plays. They cover a wide range of types and classes: a queen, a countess, princesses, dukes' daughters, a doctor's daughter, merchants' daughters, ladies-in-waiting, servants, shepherdesses, a goat-girl, nuns and prostitutes. This rich variety gives tremendous scope for contrasts and comparisons among the women themselves, as well as between men and women. With the exception of *The Tempest*, in which Miranda is the only woman, the other comedies present women as foils to each other. At its best, use of this device not only results in the idiosyncrasies of speech and behaviour, which make the heroines so very alive and credible, but also allows Shakespeare to reveal many subtle facets of their natures.

The three earliest comedies, *The Comedy of Errors*, *The Two Gentlemen of Verona* and *Love's Labours Lost*, are not marked by great subtlety in the presentation of any of their characters. *The Comedy of Errors* is a farce. It has a swiftly-moving plot and the laughs come from seeing the characters getting stuck in the hoops of various highly improbable situations until they all land on their feet at the end, to our applause. The complicated problems set before us are: will Ægeon be executed and will he find his identical twin sons (both named Antipholus) who have been separated since they were babies, each with an identical twin servant (both named Dromio)? Shakespeare has added an interesting ingredient to the cavortings of the plot in the person of Adriana, wife to Antipholus of Ephesus. Whereas characterisation of the two Antipholuses and the two Dromios is minimal (their likeness in personality as well as appearance heightens the confusion and thus the comedy), Adriana emerges with a definite identity of her own. It is not explored so deeply as to turn interest away from the central concerns of the play, but from the first she exhibits a particular characteristic that sets her apart from the rest.

Adriana's special trait is jealousy, so much so that she is virtually a portrait of the disease, causing her sister to upbraid her: 'Self-harming jealousy! Fie! beat it hence.' But Adriana cannot get rid of it. She is seething because her husband is late for dinner and she feeds her fury with jealous imaginings:

> I know his eye doth homage otherwhere,
> Or else what lets it but he would be here?
> (II.i. 104–5)

Thoughts of the woman she is increasingly sure he is visiting also make her jealous of youth and beauty, blaming her loss of both on her husband:

> Hath homely age the alluring beauty took
> From my cheek? Then, he hath wasted it.
> (II.i. 89–90)

She refuses to accept her sister's commonsense suggestions as to why Antipholus may be delayed, but instead her possessive love of him makes her certain of the worst. Ironically, when she locks her true husband out, having mistaken Antipholus of Syracuse for him, he does go and have dinner with another woman, a courtesan. He then declares that Adriana's jealous accusations have often been flung at him before, but that until now he was innocent. Adriana's jealousy, thus proved baseless up until the moment when her actions *caused* Antipholus to go to the courtesan, has a profound effect on her whole personality. She is jealous of men's liberty compared with the servitude of women, and is therefore clearly revealed as 'unnatural'. Her domineering personality and carping tongue are shown throughout the play in contrast with the patient, sober figure of Luciana, her sister, who voices all the 'correct' views. For instance, when Adriana longs for more freedom, Luciana is quick to remind her:

> Why, headstrong liberty is lash'd with woe.
> There's nothing situate under heaven's eye
> But hath his bound, in earth, in sea, in sky
> The beasts, the fishes and the winged fowls
> Are their male's subjects and at their control.
> (II.i. 15–19)

Her anxiety to preserve the *status quo* takes a strange turn when later she counsels the Antipholus she believes to be Adriana's husband, to keep up the appearance of loving his wife, even if he only married her for her money:

> Look sweet, speak fair, become disloyalty;
> Apparel vice like virtue's harbinger.
> (III.ii. 11–12)

Her words spring from her loyalty to her sister, but although Antipholus may be deceived as to their basic immorality and fall in love with this

25 The character of Adriana, here played by Judi Dench, is a study in jealousy. Luciana
is played by Francesca Annis, 1977

'dear creature', we are not and, as a result, Luciana's character fails to convince. Her prime function in the play is to act as a foil to Adriana.

The idea that in some way it is Adriana's own fault, that she is deceived and hurt because of the corrupting force of jealousy, is vital. Otherwise we might become too involved and sympathetic with her, for although possessive, her love for Antipholus is shown as genuine. Once she is face to face with him her anger abates and she is willing to forgive him 'a thousand idle pranks'. The fact that she is addressing the wrong Antipholus doesn't diminish our response to the integrity of her feeling, instead we move dangerously close to seeing the deception as unjust. Much later in the play, when Adriana has suffered more indignities and been told by the courtesan of her husband's lies, her love transcends her desire to punish him. It is most dramatically shown in the scene in which she thinks he is about to fight with the Merchant and her first, instinctive cry is: 'Hold! Hurt him not, for God's sake!' The pathos of her position is increased when, almost immediately afterwards, Adriana is made to see the error of her ways. When the Abbess insists that Antipholus' strange behaviour came as the direct result of her jealousy, she is unable to defend herself. Her humble comment on the Abbess' words is: 'She did betray me to my own reproof.'

Such introspection and self-discovery is not the stuff of comedy. It lasts only a moment before the audience is back on safe ground with Adriana demanding that the Abbess release her husband. Interest in her as an individual now diminishes; she is reconciled to her husband and her place as his wife. Her only function now is to help unravel the mysteries of the past twenty-four hours for the benefit of the other characters. In the last moments of the play it is the Abbess who assumes the greatest importance among the women characters. Not only is she revealed to be Ægeon's wife, thus putting the last piece into the symmetrical mosaic of relationships at the end, but she is the principal agent of restored order. Her penetrating comments reform Adriana and she brings twins, father and twin servants together at last.

With *The Two Gentlemen of Verona* we move away from the comedy of situation to the comedy of appearance and reality. It is soon obvious that of the two who appear to be gentlemen, Proteus is no gentleman at all but a traitor to both friendship and love. He deceives Valentine, a true friend, 'a gentleman and well derived', and casts aside his old love, Julia, in order to pursue Silvia, Valentine's beloved. The psychology of these re-

lationships, and the pattern of betrayal, forgiveness and final reconciliation is hard to swallow. Most distasteful of all is when Valentine, in proof
of friendship and forgiveness, tells Proteus (who a moment earlier has
considered raping Silvia) 'All that was mine in Silvia I give thee'. Not
only does this make a nonsense of Valentine's much-vaunted love for
Silvia, but she herself is standing with him as he says it and is allowed no
reaction. She has suddenly been reduced to a mere cipher in the final resolution of the plot. When her father, the Duke of Milan, ultimately
grants her to Valentine (Proteus in the meantime having rediscovered
Julia and his love for her), Silvia still makes no comment. Valentine's
stilted reply—'I thank your Grace; the gift hath made me happy'—is
laughably inadequate, given that he has been hotly pursuing her since
Act II. The scene—and the play—then finishes without another word
from Silvia. What has happened in the last minutes is that Valentine
offered her to Proteus, but Proteus passed her over in favour of Julia,
remarking discourteously in her hearing:

> What is in Silvia's face, but I may spy
> More fresh in Julia's . . .?
> (V.iv. 112–13)

Thurio, earlier a rival for Silvia's love, appeared and claimed her, but
was warned off by Valentine. Cowed, Thurio immediately declared that
he did not want her. The Duke applauded Valentine's spirit and gave
her to him. One might explain Silvia's silence as the most effective way of
conveying her shock at being rejected in rapid succession by three men,
and then firmly handed back to one of them by her father, but that would
be forcing an interpretation on the text. One has no choice but to see the
ending of *The Two Gentlemen of Verona* as highly unsatisfactory in terms of
Silvia's characterisation.

Earlier, Silvia was presented as an idealised image of female beauty
and accomplishment: men fall in love with her on sight, vie for her
favours and find her merits inexpressible:

> Then to Silvia let us sing,
> That Silvia is excelling;
> She excels each mortal thing
> Upon the dull earth dwelling.
> (IV.ii. 48–51)

Such awe-struck commonplaces, together with the catalogue of her
virtues given by Valentine and Proteus, are not promising as the basis

26 The ring on her finger betrays Julia, for her faithless lover Proteus now sees through her disguise as a page in *Two Gentlemen of Verona*. Helen Mirren and Ian Richardson as Julia and Proteus, 1970

for a character study. She would remain simply a pivot for the plot were it not for the emergence of her true voice in Act IV. Here she berates Proteus for his disloyalty and by doing so becomes the voice of truth and good judgement in the play. Her severe answer to his amorous pleading is:

> Thou subtle, perjur'd, false, disloyal man!
> Thinkst thou I am so shallow, so conceitless
> To be seduced by thy flattery?
> > (IV.ii. 94–6)

Her sensitivity and integrity are further evident when Julia, disguised as his page, brings Proteus' ring as a gift to her—the very ring that Julia herself gave him before he left for Milan:

Silvia: The more shame for him that he sends it me;
  For I have heard him say a thousand times,
  His Julia gave it him at his departure.

Thou his false finger have profan'd the ring,
Mine shall not do his Julia so much wrong.
(IV.iv. 138–42)

Silvia's virtue and constancy shine out in her words and her behaviour, for she repulses Proteus on moral grounds and is prepared to brave any dangers in order to be with Valentine. In this she functions as a further contrast to the faithless behaviour of Proteus himself.

Her foil, Julia, is a prototype of comic heroines in the later plays. The relationship with her waiting-woman Lucetta foreshadows that of Portia and Nerissa in *The Merchant of Venice* for she is Julia's confidante and witty counsellor. Their catechismic exchanges early in the play are tedious to modern tastes and do little to reveal character but the relationship has a moment of credibility when Julia begs Lucetta to help her plan 'a journey to my loving Proteus' in Milan. Lucetta's fears for her mistress's safety in the face of Julia's determination to go, create a fine tension. Once Julia has decided to travel in disguise as a page, her waiting-woman is swept along by her enthusiasm and the subsequent banter reflects the affectionate, informal regard between them:

Lucetta: What fashion, madam, shall I make your breeches?
Julia: That fits as well as 'Tell me, good my lord,
            What compass will you wear your farthingale?'
                                    (II.vii. 49–51)

Julia is the first of Shakespeare's comic heroines to be allowed the device of disguise, a device he used with great effect for Portia and Viola. We do not see much of Julia as Proteus' page, but there is sufficient to create painful ironies, particularly when he sends her to Silvia with the ring. So Julia says 'How many women would do such a message?' and rationalises

Because he loves her, he despiseth me;
Because I love him, I must pity him!
                                    (IV.iv. 100–1)

In spite of such indications in *The Two Gentlemen of Verona* that Shakespeare is moving towards a more compelling characterisation for his women, in the third of these early comedies he is still very much concerned with surface issues.

Love's Labours Lost is notorious for the number of academic and 'Elizabethan' jokes it contains, most of which are lost on a modern audience. It also has a more scholarly subject than the other comedies: what happens when man defies the laws of nature? The King of Navarre, with the eager acquiescence of his lords, passes an absurd decree that for three years no member of his court shall see a woman. He and his three lord-attendants swear to obey the edict, but are immediately put to the test by the arrival of the Princess of France and her three ladies-in-waiting, and the play chronicles their consequent failure to keep their bond and proves to the chastened Navarre and his friends that man cannot fight his true nature.

The instruments of their self-revelation are the Princess of France and her ladies, whose clear-eyed commonsense is constantly shown in contrast with the blind conceit of the men. The Princess in particular is presented as shrewd and straightforward, quick to identify exaggeration and deception even when it is intended to please her. Here she counters her own attendant, Boyet, who has flattered her:

> my beauty, though but mean,
> Needs not the painted flourish of your praise.
> (II.i. 13–14)

Her ladies, Rosaline, Maria and Katherine, are equally forthright, their words, like those of their princess, laced with wit. As Boyet remarks:

> The tongues of mocking wenches are as keen
> As is the razor's edge invisible.
> (V.ii. 256–7)

An interesting aspect of the contrast these four make with the men is their loyalty to, and openness with, each other. The King of Navarre and his lords have to conceal their love, and thus deceive each other as well as break their oaths. Whereas the Princess can share her delight with her ladies that 'we are wise girls to mock our lovers so', these self-same lovers have suffered as much from the need to keep their affections secret as from the snubs and jibes of the women. The group of women has a cohesion and stability not apparent among the men, and also their actions condition the progress of the plot. Whatever plans the men lay are disrupted in some sense when put to the test. Even at the end, when circumstances have stripped the now-humbled lovers of strategy and left them with only 'honest plain words' to plead their causes, the women leave them with an ultimatum. Each man will have to spend a year doing suitable penance in order to prove that his oath of love can bind him more strongly than his oath of abstinence. As Berowne wryly remarks:

27 The Princess of France ultimately proves to the King of Navarre that man cannot fight his true nature in *Love's Labours Lost*. Charles Kay and Glenda Jackson, 1965

> Our wooing doth not end like an old play,
> Jack hath not Jill; these ladies' courtesy
> Might well have made our sport a comedy.
> (V.ii. 863–5)

The play is very close, if not to tragedy, at least to something other than comedy. It is kept within the comic mode, contrary to Berowne's opinion, because the confusions and intricacies of the plot are smoothed out at the end, the language is light and witty, and there is the promise of happiness, even though it is not achieved within the bounds of the play.

With *A Midsummer Night's Dream* we again find a royal court as the setting for diversion and laughter, but the feeling there is very different from the strained and claustrophobic atmosphere of the Court of Navarre.

For Theseus, Duke of Athens, love's labours have already been won for he is to marry Hippolyta, Queen of the Amazons, and preparations for their wedding form the framework of the play. The plot-structure is ambitious, involving four clearly differentiated groups of characters: Theseus, Hippolyta and their court, a group of Athenians quarrelling over a marriage, craftsmen and fairies. The four groups are principally linked by the activities of Puck, 'a knavish sprite', but another welding force is the contrast and comparison between the characters themselves.

In a play almost certainly written to celebrate a marriage, it is not surprising to find marriage and marital relationships as important themes. Hippolyta, the bride for whose benefit holiday, feast and entertainment are proclaimed in Athens, has only a small part in the play and no part at all in the development of the plot. As Shakespeare's audience would have known, she had been the proud queen of the warlike Amazons who were defeated by Theseus in battle. Theseus admits to her:

> I woo'd thee with my sword,
> And won thy love doing thee injuries.
> (I.i. 16–17)

The only aspect of her personality revealed is her total submission to Theseus. She speaks few lines and is in essence a static figure, symbolic of the joyful but humble bride. In complete contrast we have Hermia and Helena, very much alive and most unhappy about their marriage-prospects.

Within moments of the start of the play, Theseus' gentle words to Hippolyta are interrupted by Hermia's father, intent on forcing his daughter to marry the young Athenian Demetrius. Demetrius is eager enough, but Hermia spurns him for Lysander. Her friend Helena was once courted by Demetrius, with whom she is still in love. The fortunes of these four occupy much of the play, and the personalities of the two women are contrasted and compared.

Hermia and Helena are presented in parallel terms. They are the same age, having studied at school together, and have had a close, affectionate friendship. When she thinks that Hermia is mocking her, Helena holds up this earlier friendship as an ideal now betrayed:

> We, Hermia, like two artificial gods,
> Have with our neelds[1] created both one flower,
> Both on one sampler, sitting on one cushion,

[1] *neelds*: needles.

86

Both warbling of one song, both in one key,
As if our hands, our sides, voices and minds,
Had been incorporable. So we grew together,
Like to a double cherry, seeming parted,
But yet an union in partition,
Two lovely berries moulded on one stem.
                    (III.ii. 203–11)

The constant pairing, culminating in the exquisite image of the double cherry, emphasises their similarity, in education and taste. Helena's claims are borne out by the general likenesses of character and behaviour discernible throughout the play. Both of them are witty and honest, as evident with Hermia from the instant she opens her mouth. It is clear that she is not just a puppet-figure, obedient to the whims of her father or the rival lovers. Theseus has told her that she should obey her father and marry Demetrius, who is a worthy suitor. 'So is Lysander,' comes Hermia's quick response. She, like Helena, is true to her feelings and not prepared to deny them or be beaten down, even by a Duke. The two are also linked by naïvety. Hermia joins with Lysander in telling Helena of their plan to elope, without considering for a moment that Helena might use the information for her own devices. Similarly Helena rushes off to tell Demetrius, deluding herself that he will thank her for it. In the final resolution of the love-tangle, Hermia and Helena are once again in perfect balance, each with the man she loves.

If this were all that there was to their portrayal we would be looking at two female Antipholuses, interesting only for their function in the unfolding of the plot. Their personalities are brought alive for us by other means. Not only do their speeches have a directness and colloquial quality that infuses them with life, but there are differences between them.

First of all they are placed in changing, contrasting situations until Puck resolves their dilemma. When Demetrius and Lysander are both in love with Hermia, Helena is consistently shown as envious of Hermia's attractiveness. Alone in the wood she muses:

Happy is Hermia, wheresoe'er she lies;
For she hath blessed and attractive eyes.
How came her eyes so bright? Not with salt tears:
If so, my eyes are oftener wash'd than hers.
No, no, I am as ugly as a bear.
                    (II.ii. 89–93)

There is an unmistakable ring of psychological truth: the wretched Helena finds herself totally despicable—'ugly as a bear'—in comparison with Hermia, because no matter what she does, she cannot win Demetrius. When the tables are turned and both men desert Hermia, Helena has been so long rejected that she is unable to believe them:

> O spite! O hell! I see you all are bent
> To set against me for your merriment:
> (III.ii. 145–6)

Her self-pity turns into fury, which she vents not only on the men, but also on Hermia whom she believes to be in league with them. The consequent exchange of insults is, for its comic-value, one of the high spots of the play. What is more, it helps us see further differences between the two women, for each fastens on some characteristic of the other to use as a taunt. Hermia sees a remark of Helena's as an implication that she is short. It is evidently a sensitive point, for she becomes enraged:

> How low am I, thou painted maypole? Speak;
> How low am I? I am not yet so low
> But that my nails can reach unto thine eyes.
> (III.ii. 296–8)

Yet the dialogue is not so evenly matched in tone and insult as to lose impact by being unreal. Helena's anger never reaches the heights of Hermia's, and in the middle of the quarrel Helena makes an impassioned plea:

> Good Hermia, do not be so bitter with me.
> I evermore did love you, Hermia,
> Did ever keep your counsels, never wrong'd you;
> (III.ii. 306–8)

By the end of their altercation we have a clear sense of them as individuals: Hermia short, aggressive and unrelenting; Helena tall, anguished and a coward physically. The definition of their characters is conveyed so forcefully that it remains with us, even though they have only a few more lines in the play and none of any great significance. Once

---

28 Titania quarrels with Oberon in *A Midsummer Night's Dream*, and she is punished for her presumption by being made to look foolish. Vivien Leigh, 1937

the correct balance has been established between the two pairs of lovers, Hermia and Helena retire into the background like Hippolyta, and let their men do the talking.

There is another female figure in *A Midsummer Night's Dream*: Titania. Although described as 'Queen of the Fairies', she is given credibility by being shown with very human traits (unlike Puck, for instance, who is wholly fairy). The most important aspect of Titania's character is her relationship with her husband Oberon, and in this she provides another facet of the marriage-theme. She and Oberon quarrel over the possession of an Indian boy, for Oberon is jealous that Titania should keep him as her 'henchman'. They are unable to resolve their quarrel and so Oberon determines to trick Titania and force her to give in. He tells us: 'I'll make her render up her page to me.' His plan is completely successful. Titania is made to look foolish by falling in love with Bottom transformed into an ass, and while still in her enchanted state, freely giving the boy to Oberon. Titania has no chance to fight the magic and when she is released from its power, all thought of the child also vanishes. Harmony is restored, for as Oberon says: 'Now thou and I are new in amity.'

What is interesting is the tacit assumption that Oberon's behaviour is justified. In the initial wrangle over the boy there was no indication that Oberon had a superior claim, indeed Titania appeared to have more right, since she was fulfilling an obligation to the child's mother (II.i. 123–37). But Shakespeare makes it clear that nothing Titania can claim or do will justify the fundamental wrong she has committed: she has failed to submit to her husband's desires. To an Elizabethan audience she would appear both foolish and arrogant in her quarrel with Oberon, for punishment was bound to follow. Her 'crime' was particularly heinous because, as Queen of the Fairies, she should exemplify the characteristics of the ideal human wife, which did not include rebellion. In keeping with the social conventions of the time Titania's downfall is therefore inevitable. The audience joins with Oberon in laughing at her ridiculous infatuation with Bottom, applauding her return to sanity and thereby concurring with the idea that Oberon had every right to trick her. In this way Titania is linked with Hippolyta, not merely by her social position as first lady in a hierarchy, but because both have had to give in to their lords. Although Helena and Hermia did not give in to theirs, there is a suggestion at the end of the play that male-dominance is important here also. Once the four lovers have been satisfactorily paired off, Hermia and Helena virtually disappear from the play. They are

29 The scene where Titania is infatuated with Bottom in Peter Brook's remarkable production of *A Midsummer Night's Dream*, 1970

present at the entertainment provided for Theseus and Hippolyta, but it is Demetrius and Lysander who talk about the craftsmen's efforts. The women become the conservative, sixteenth-century ideal: submissive and silent.

Not so Portia. With *The Merchant of Venice* we move away from the moonlit fairytale ambience of the woods near Athens, to the harsher light of what is perhaps the most sententious of all the comedies. It is concerned with moral truths and the conflicts that arise when different sets of values are set against each other. The plot has three elements: the wooing and winning of Portia, the downfall of Shylock in court, and the revelation to their husbands that Portia and her maid were the lawyer and clerk instrumental in Shylock's ruin. Portia herself is the lynch-pin for each of these episodes, and she is remarkable among Shakespeare's heroines for being a dominant character throughout the play as well as so constantly vital to the plot. She does not share this position with another woman of equal status, like Hermia and Helena or the pairs in the later comedies. Nerissa, her waiting-woman, is her confidante and thereby her foil in the sense that they can talk as women together, but Nerissa does not really have an existence or power of her own, separate from those of her mistress.

The great moment and surprise of the play is Portia's appearance as a doctor of law at the trial of Shylock *v.* Antonio, who has failed to repay money borrowed and must therefore comply with the bond he signed, allowing Shylock to cut out a pound of his flesh. It is worth pausing a moment to consider just what Shakespeare is doing here. The comic device of a woman dressed as a boy was used in *Two Gentlemen of Verona* and will appear again in *As You Like It* and *Twelfth Night*. In each of these plays, the woman uses disguise to get close to her lover and it liberates her and allows her to prove her worth. Portia has no need to do that. She already has a doting husband and her disguise has only an indirect association with her romantic interests (Antonio had borrowed the money in order to lend it to Bassanio so that he could woo her). The reason for her appearance in court, dressed as a man, reveals Shakespeare suggesting something very daring. There are two important facts about the court case: it was unquestionably settled because of Portia's brilliant handling of legal technicalities, and she would never have been allowed to speak had it been known that she was a woman. The implication is that Portia had the best mind of those present, better than that of her social superior the Duke and better than that of her husband. What is more, she does not retreat, as the women in the comedies so frequently do once all is settled in the final act. Portia remains the directing and organising force until the last.

One wonders how this phenomenon, the powerful, intelligent woman, could be credible to an Elizabethan audience. It would seem that apart from exemplifying some of the virtues of Queen Elizabeth herself, Portia represents that rare creature, a woman of independent means. She is subject to the caprices of her father in that his will stipulates that her future husband will be the one who can choose correctly among three caskets, but there is no man actually present to oversee the terms of the marriage. Portia is faithful to her dead father's wishes, but she makes all other decisions herself. When Bassanio learns, just at the moment he has won her, that Shylock has demanded his pound of flesh from Antonio, it is Portia who makes the decisions for him, that he must marry her and then leave at once to aid Antonio. The intellectual as well as the commanding side of her nature is clear from the outset. In the amusing exchange with Nerissa (I.ii) in which she chronicles her dislike of all her suitors, she is frequently tempted into philosophical ruminations. At one point she briskly interrupts herself with: 'But this reasoning is not in the fashion to choose me a husband.' Even in the tense moment before her beloved Bassanio attempts the casket-test, Portia cannot resist exploring the possibilities of word-play:

> Beshrew your eyes,
> They have o'erlook'd me and divided me:
> One half of me is yours, the other half yours,
> Mine own, I would say; but if mine then yours,
> And so all yours.
> (III.ii. 14–18)

It is no wonder that the simple Bassanio responds desperately:

> let me choose;
> For as I am, I live upon the rack.
> (III.ii. 24–5)

Portia's character is carefully and consistently drawn, and so her amazing talents in the court room come as a surprise, but not a shock. After Shylock has disappeared from the play there is a marked change in tone, for the emphasis now is on the happy love between Portia and Bassanio, Nerissa and Gratiano, and Shylock's daughter, Jessica, and

30 The powerful figure of Portia dominates the courtroom scene in *The Merchant of Venice*. Here she is played by Violet Vanbrugh, in 1905

Lorenzo. Portia remains true to form however, and passes stern judgement on both her husband and Nerissa's for giving away their rings, as they thought, to the 'lawyer' and his 'clerk'. It is all a great joke, of course, for we know that at any moment Portia and Nerissa will reveal the truth. Even so, the scene is characterised by the serious tone of the rebukes and consequent oaths of fidelity sworn penitently by Bassanio and Gratiano. We are left with a feeling of great admiration for Portia, that she can organise her life and others' so well, but it is tempered by the realisation that she becomes impassioned only in argument, and there is virtually no softer, more lyrical side to her. She does not provoke tender concern for her fiery vulnerability like a Hermia or a Helena.

'Fiery' would certainly apply to the temperament of Katharina in *The Taming of the Shrew*. Her taming, and particularly her last speech where she effectively shakes off her old personality to become her husband's slave, have excited strong reactions from modern audiences and critics. George Bernard Shaw was moved to write:

> ... the last scene is altogether disgusting to modern sensibility. No man with any decency of feeling can sit it out in the company of a woman without being extremely ashamed of the lord-of-creation moral implied in the wager and the speech put into the woman's own mouth.
>
> (*Saturday Review*, 6 November, 1897)

Shaw felt Petruchio's treatment of Katharina was a repugnant and progressive demoralisation of what had been a high-spirited young woman. To see if there is a basis for Shaw's criticism we need to look closely at the kind of characterisation meted out to the 'intolerable curst and shrewd and froward' heroine.

The play is not altogether cohesive in structure, being a play-within-a-play arranged for Christopher Sly, a tinker who was carried while dead drunk to a nobleman's house. Here he was made to believe, on returning to consciousness, that he was a wealthy lord just recovered from a long fit of insanity. A group of wandering players 'are come to play a pleasant comedy' supposedly to aid Sly's rapid return to health, but really at the bidding of the nobleman to provoke more laughter among his men at Sly's expense. During the course of the play there is a short interruption from Sly in Act I, but after that his presence is forgotten. There is no return to the gallery for comment at the end and so *The Taming Of The Shrew* is really only a play-within-half-a-play.

Directors have been known to leave the Christopher Sly episode out altogether, but if we allow that it was Shakespeare's intention to create a frame, or part of a frame, for the story of Katharina and Petruchio, such omission seems cavalier. The closer focus also means that the content of the play is harsher and has to be taken entirely on its own merits. The tone established in the Induction prepares us for the possibility of farce, with minimal characterisation—although after such promise the play comes as a pleasant surprise with its lively protagonists—but a failure to appreciate the significance of the Induction leads to a view of the play more stringent than perhaps it merits.

Such considerations do not entirely account for or excuse the treatment meted out to Katharina. In terms of the plot, her interests are secondary to those of her painfully insipid younger sister Bianca (who cannot get married until Katharina has found a husband), and at first there is the sense that despite her bravado she is merely a pawn. One of the few moments of true characterisation comes when Katharina, seeing Bianca's interests favoured above her own, exclaims with pain and passion to her father:

> Nay, now I see
> She is your treasure, she must have a husband;
> I must dance barefoot on her wedding-day,
> And, for your love to her, lead apes in hell.
> Talk not to me: I will go sit and weep.
> (II.i. 31–5)

Such personal revelations are rare. Katharina is never allowed a soliloquy and so we cannot learn her innermost thoughts. It is true that her character does change radically during the course of the play, but we observe it externally, through the comments of other characters and as a *fait accompli* in Katharina herself. She exhibits the stereotyped characteristics of the 'shrewish' woman: violent behaviour, coarse language and a total disregard of authority. We are delighted by her vivid, energetic speech and her audacity when she threatens Hortensio, who has cracked jokes at her expense, that she would like 'to comb your noddle with a three legg'd stool' (I.i. 64), or when she bandies vulgarities with Petruchio:

> *Petruchio.* Who knows not where a wasp does wear his sting?
> In his tail.
> *Katharina.* In his tongue.
> *Pet.* Whose tongue?

31 Katharina (Edith Evans) is forced to leave her wedding feast and unceremoniously carried off by Petruchio (Leslie Banks) to his country house, 1937

Kath.	Yours, if you talk of tails; and so farewell.
Pet.	What! With my tongue in your tail? Nay; come again. Good Kate, I am a gentleman.
Kath.	That I'll try. [*Striking him*]

(II.i. 214–29)

This is not to say that we can comprehend or sympathise with her character; we are simply knocked over by the anarchic power she unleashes. As Petruchio steadily and triumphantly out-shrews the shrew, this force abates in her until she has been cowed into total submissiveness. By the end of the play she does exemplify the sixteenth-century ideal of an adoring, concurring wife, but the very stereotyping of the two extremes of her behaviour suggests that Shakespeare may not have intended us to take her case altogether seriously. There is a pleasant irony, also, in that the faultless Bianca exhibits alarmingly shrewish tendencies in the final scene. She and Katharina effectively change places, for the infamous 'lord-of-creation' speech censured by Shaw, is in part directed at her. Perhaps Shakespeare is suggesting that there is a hint of shrewishness in all women.

Helena, heroine of *All's Well That Ends Well*, is like Katharina, in that she goes beyond the bounds of behaviour acceptable in a woman. Unlike Katharina, however, Helena's actions are praiseworthy and she is shown to be consciously adopting her 'unfeminine' role because it is the only way in which her husband, Bertram, can be brought to his senses. She woos him, but once he sees the error of his ways she immediately becomes the passive partner. It is difficult to forgive Helena for falling in love with such a boorish, spoilt and self-deceiving man as Bertram. The New Cambridge Shakespeare is unequivocal in condemning *All's Well That Ends Well* as 'Shakespeare's worst play', partly for this reason and partly for the tedious plot, and the sequence of events certainly does at times seem contrived and needlessly digressive. Surprisingly in this unpromising setting both Helena and the other important woman in the play, the Countess of Rousillon, have a fair measure of individuality, although it fades in the latter part of the play.

Helena states her problem and the central preoccupation of the play in her first speech:

32 At the end of *The Taming of the Shrew*, Katharina is 'tamed' into the Elizabethan ideal of the adoring, compliant wife. Michael Williams as Petruchio and Janet Suzman as Katharina, 1967

there is no living, none,
If Bertram be away. It were all one
That I should love a bright particular star
And think to wed it, he is so above me.

(I.i. 87–90)

It is not that she lacks beauty, virtue or even opportunity, but rather that as a mere physician's daughter she comes from the wrong class to marry a Count. Her love, coupled with encouragement from Bertram's mother, the Countess, steels her resolution to follow Bertram to the King's court. She cures the king of an ulcer and in return is allowed to choose any man she wishes as her husband. Bertram (for of course her choice lights on him) responds with a brutal rejection of Helena, publicly denoucing her. Even when the king offers to give her wealth and a title, Bertram remains sullenly obdurate: 'I cannot love her, nor will strive to do't.' Helena has stayed silent since the Count's first outburst against her. His sneering at her lowly birth provokes no response and it is only when he rejects her on an emotional level by saying that he will not *love* her that she is stung to the quick. The reticence of her interruption, as if she can hardly bear to utter the words, telling the king that she will withdraw her claim, has a ring of psychological truth and engages our sympathy. Another instance when her anguish is effectively conveyed comes when Helena parts from Bertram who has been forced by the king to marry her. To his terse and unkind: 'What would you have?' she replies with a combination of modesty and courage that betrays her vulnerability:

Something, and scarce so much: nothing, indeed.
I would not tell you what I would, my lord:
Faith, yes;
Strangers and foes do sunder and not kiss.

(II.v. 85–8)

It takes the whole four lines to get to the vital word, reflecting Helena's agony at having to beg the husband whom she loves so much to kiss her.

The episode involving the 'bed-trick' is less convincing, for the contortions of the plot overtake the need for subtle characterisation. Helena's character loses sharp definition once she is paralleled with Julia, another virtuous woman who is deceived by Bertram. The 'bed-trick' itself has the effect of further easing Helena out of our sympathies, for it is proof that her goodness cannot prevail against Bertram's cruelty and snobbishness on its own. Mechanical means have to be introduced, weakening the plot and firmly establishing Helena and Julia as co-agents in its unravelling. Their interests are subordinated and they cease to have any credibility as characters in their own right.

The Countess suffers something of the same fate. At first she has an important role because she is the principal source of information about Helena and the unimpeachable proof of her moral excellence. She encourages Helena to follow Bertram and approves of her love, for her affection for Helena is such that she tells her:

33 In *All's Well that Ends Well*, Helena is rejected by her boorish husband Bertram. As Mrs Warren's portrayal suggests, she is a lonely, holy woman, not always convincing as a character, 1785

> I am your mother;
> And put you in the catalogue of those
> That were enwombed mine.
>
> (I.iii. 145–7)

This loving indulgence towards her son and Helena is the Countess' most obvious characteristic and conditions her responses. She is able neither to condemn Helena for her lack of social status nor to censure Bertram for his boorish behaviour. She claims distractedly at one point:

> Which of them both
> Is dearest to me I have no skill in sense
> To make distinction.
>
> (III.iv. 38–40)

Having established beyond all doubt that Helena is the ideal wife for Bertram had he but the wit to see it, the Countess' function in the play is essentially at an end. She lingers on through the last three acts in scenes of little substance. In the final moments of Act V, when Helena confronts Bertram and he acknowledges her worth, she turns to the Countess and says: 'O my dear mother; do I see you living?' The Countess does not answer, but we care so little about her by this time that her silence passes unnoticed.

The other play amongst the comedies to use the heroine as the instrument of redemption for a morally deficient man is *Measure for Measure*. Like Helena, Isabella has to resort to the 'bed-trick' in order to achieve her aim, but the device is dove-tailed into the plot far more neatly than in *All's Well That Ends Well*.

Isabella is supreme amongst Shakespeare's heroines as a symbol of chastity and purity, for she is about to enter an enclosed order of nuns. Her longing for a life of material privation in order to concentrate on spiritual matters is immediately apparent where she is shown around the nunnery:

> Isabella.   And have you nuns no further privileges?
> Francisca. Are not these large enough?
> Isab.   Yes, truly: I speak not as desiring more,
>   But rather wishing a more strict restraint
>   Upon the sisterhood.
>
> (I.iv. 1–5)

Her virtue is unqualified by any human weakness, for she does not even

102

suffer the pangs of love, unlike that other model of moral excellence, Helena. There is a chill quality in her that at first overawes, but ultimately tires, us. She does not truly seem a thing of flesh and blood. As the dandy Lucio says in an aside to her: 'You are too cold.'

Isabella's brother, Claudio, has made a girl, Juliet, pregnant. A new law requires that any man found guilty of fornication must be beheaded, and Claudio is to be used as an example to others. He is guilty, but there are mitigating circumstances: he loves her and would have married her had there not been formal problems about her dowry. Isabella pleads for his life with Angelo, the lord Deputy, who offers Claudio's life in exchange for 'the treasures of your body'. The cowardly Claudio begs her to agree to the demand but Isabella refuses, for 'More than our brother is our chastity'. Ultimately she agrees to a bed-trick with Mariana, a woman rejected by Angelo after he had promised to marry her because her dowry was lost. In case we question Isabella's morality we are told firmly that 'the doubleness of the benefit defends the deceit from reproof' (III.i. 265–6). Angelo's villainy is revealed, but he is forgiven and marries Mariana. Claudio is released and made to promise to marry Juliet, and the Duke of Vienna, who arranges all this and had suggested the bed-trick as a solution, is clearly in love with Isabella.

Isabella's function in the play is both to make her brother recognise his cowardice and to be the instrument of reconciliation between Angelo and Mariana by exposing Angelo's hypocrisy. Her motivation in both cases is a strong sense of moral duty. There is no hint of self-interest in her actions and this is another feature that sets her apart from other leading women in the comedies. The Duke's suggestion of marriage comes as a surprise: there has been nothing to suggest that Isabella wishes to marry him, or indeed wishes to marry at all. Her character is clearly shown to be better adapted to the cool walks of the cloister than the fluctuating emotional temperatures of the outside world. Even so, there are some marvellous moments in her dialogues with Angelo and her brother. She is shown capable of an impassioned intellectualism as here, where she berates the lord Deputy:

> man, proud man,
> Drest in a little brief authority,
> Most ignorant of what he's most assur'd,
> His glassy essence, like an angry ape,
> Plays such fantastic tricks before high heaven
> As make the angels weep.
> (II.ii. 117–22)

34 The most saintly figure amongst Shakespeare's heroines is Isabella, who is about to enter a nunnery when she becomes embroiled in her brother's misdemeanours. Lily Brayton as Isabella in 1906

The sheer force of the language and its extraordinary imagery prevent the speech from becoming sanctimonious.

Another side of her is revealed when Claudio pleads that she give in to Angelo. Isabella has had absolute faith in her brother's integrity:

> had he twenty heads to tender down
> On twenty bloody blocks, he'd yield them up,
> Before his sister should her body stoop
> To such abhorr'd pollution.
>
> (II.iv. 180–3)

Her reaction to his betrayal of her trust is immediate and violent; to her, justice and virtue are inseparable:

> O faithless coward! O dishonest wretch!
> Wilt thou be made a man out of my vice?
> Is't not a kind of incest, to take life
> From thine own sister's shame?
>
> (III.i. 136–9)

As proper for one intending to become a nun, death holds no terrors for her. She is even able to see it as a desirable release, for on hearing of Angelo's harsh treatment of Mariana, her first thought is: 'What a merit were it in death to take this poor maid from the world.' Isabella is certainly far more convincing than Helena, her closest counterpart, but our prevailing impression is of an aloof, daunting figure, too remote to engage our sympathy.

There is a Claudio in *Much Ado About Nothing*, but his name is the only resemblance this play has to *Measure for Measure*. Together with *As You Like It* and *Twelfth Night*, the two other plays written between 1598 and 1600, *Much Ado* represents the height of Shakespeare's achievement in the comedies, not least because of the compelling characters of the women.

There are two heroines in the play, but their roles are very different. So far as the plot is concerned, Hero is the more important, for it is her relationship with Claudio that conditions the action throughout. He woos her, wins her and nearly marries her but for a trick played on him whereby he is convinced that she is unchaste. He shames her by accusing her in the church, but after various further deceptions and revelations, realises his error and they are reunited. In view of all this, it comes as a surprise to realise that although Hero frequently appears in the first four acts, she rarely says anything. Our information about her worth and beauty comes from others, and plans for her marriage to Claudio are made without our hearing any discussion that involves her opinion. When she does speak, her words are pale echoes of her cousin Beatrice's, or mild and courteous remarks to her father's guests. There is only one scene in which she comes into her own and that is when, alone with her waiting-women, Margaret and Ursula, she arranges the plot to deceive Beatrice into falling in love with Claudio's friend, Benedick. Every other time she appears she is in the company of her cousin or the men, all of whom have a dazzling command of words. Surely there is a psychological truth here, that Hero is genuinely modest in such articulate company and so does not venture to speak, except to utter a few unremarkable comments in order not to appear discourteous by offering nothing but a total silence. It is a different story with her waiting-women. Here she is the unquestioned superior and so need have no fear of being picked up on something she says and made to look foolish, as might be the case with Beatrice or Benedick. What is more, in this particular instance Hero has thought up the plan herself: it is the only moment in the play when she is galvanised into action on her own initiative. Her delight in being in sole charge of the 'false, sweet bait' that will fool her sharp, witty, dominant cousin is clearly evident when she gives strategic details to Margaret and Ursula:

> Good Margaret run thee to the parlour;
> There shalt thou find my cousin Beatrice
> Proposing with the Prince and Claudio:
> Whisper her ear, and tell her, I and Ursula
> Walk in the garden, and our whole discourse
> Is all of her; . . .
> Now, Ursula, when Beatrice doth come,
> As we do trace this alley up and down,
> Our talk must only be of Benedick:
> When I do name him, let it be thy part
> To praise him.
> (III.i. 1–6 and 15–19)

The urgency and slightly self-conscious tone of the speech suggests that Hero is not used to being an organiser. When it is clear that the plot is going to work, because Beatrice comes rushing out, surely we can detect glee as well as amusement in Hero's

35 Hero, the gentle but pallid counterpart to Beatrice in *Much Ado About Nothing*, portrayed here by Viola Tree, 1905

> Look where Beatrice, like a lapwing, runs
> Close by the ground, to hear our conference.
>   (III.i. 24–5)

In her normal behaviour it would be hard to find anyone less like the timorous lapwing than Beatrice. Hero's hopes are fulfilled: her plan has momentarily turned her cousin into a creature more shy than herself. For once Beatrice will have to do all the listening, and Hero need not fear that 'she would mock me into air'. Under the pretence that she does not know Beatrice is there, Hero can also assert her own worth in comparison with her cousin's. When she says

> So turns she every man the wrong side out
> And never gives to truth and virtue that
> Which simpleness and merit purchaseth
>   (III.i. 68–70)

surely she does so knowing that she herself is the most obvious example of 'simpleness and merit' as witnessed by Claudio's successful suit.

It is this one scene that brings Hero to life for us, and, short though it is, it compensates for, or rather, explains, all those other times when she is so unforthcoming.

Structurally speaking, the quiet, modest Hero is the perfect foil to Beatrice. They are more sophisticated versions of Bianca and Katharina in *The Taming Of The Shrew*. Although Beatrice's wit does not degenerate into the violent railing of Katharina, her personality is thrown into sharper relief by the contrast with an unassuming counterpart.

Nothing could be less like the romanticised and formal relationship of Hero and Claudio than that between Beatrice and Benedick. These two are playing a love-game, but the rules are very subtle, hidden from others in the play and, to a certain extent, even from themselves.

Beatrice is one of Shakespeare's most complex women, and her feelings for Benedick are marked by caprice and ambiguity. That, at least, is the appearance. The reality is otherwise, for the character Beatrice is a marvellous and intricately developed portrayal of self-deception through pride. We are never allowed an intense focus on the ebb and flow of her true feelings, for that would make us take her 'disability' too seriously for comedy. Shakespeare reveals the motives for her facetious and often withering remarks to Benedick by other means.

A person in love, but uncertain if that love is returned, is in a state of heightened sensitivity, and immensely vulnerable. One way of attempting to exert control over the situation is to deny that it exists, acting as though what is in reality most loved, is most despised. Such a reaction need not be conscious; it may spring as a defence against being hurt, particularly if there has been some painful rejection in the past. People with a strong intellect and forceful personality are most likely to be the victims of such self-deception, for they can rationalise away their tender feelings and coerce others into thinking that the reverse is true. Beatrice fits this pattern. She is highly intelligent and forceful, able to influence and direct others. The classic example is when Don Pedro announces to Claudio that Hero has been won, and brings the two together. One would expect this to be a great moment for Claudio and Hero, but before either has a chance to speak, Beatrice starts taking over: 'Speak, count, 'tis your cue.' In a moment she similarly directs her cousin, adding: 'or, if you cannot, stop his mouth with a kiss.' Presumably the bashful Hero does so, but that marks the end of interest being centred on her and Claudio, for now everyone starts talking about Beatrice. The woman who can so adroitly and irresistibly take over such a scene will have no trouble in persuading others to believe of her whatever she wishes, but she may be taking herself in as well.

We know that Beatrice and Benedick have been sparring partners long before the action of the play, but there are also strong hints that Beatrice has had some unsuccessful romantic involvement with him. She makes an oblique reference, in the first scene of Act I, to herself as 'my uncle's fool' who 'challenged' him on behalf of Cupid. A more positive clue is that she admits that she once had Benedick's heart but she was forced to return it to him: 'he won it of me with false dice.' She does not elaborate on what kind of trick he played, which in itself suggests that the memory is a bitter one.

The other side of the coin is that Beatrice is evidently still in love with him. Her first words in the play are to ask if he has returned safe from the wars, and she cannot stop talking about him. Leonato excuses her close questioning of the messenger by saying that 'There is a kind of merry war betwixt Signior Benedick and her', which would be exactly what Beatrice wants him to think and which she herself may well believe. When Benedick appears he does not notice Beatrice until, unable to bear his indifference any longer, but equally unable to say why, Beatrice sarcastically attacks him: 'I wonder that you will still be talking, Signior Benedick: nobody marks[2] you, (I.i. 107–8). For Benedick, the professed

[2] *marks*: notices.

man of wit, nothing could be more galling than to have it suggested that his remarks have passed unnoticed, and he is stung into a hurtful rejoinder, suggesting that he cares so little for Beatrice as to be surprised she is still alive. Beatrice replies in kind, and the pattern of insult-tennis is established, to recur almost every time they are together. Beatrice is at her sharpest when she is alone with Benedick at the end of Act II, having been sent to call him in for dinner. By this time he has been convinced through the machinations of Claudio and Don Pedro that Beatrice is in love with him, and he is eager to encourage her. The situation is not unlike the moment in *A Midsummer Night's Dream* when Demetrius suddenly tells Helena that he loves her, but because it is what she most wants to hear, she is terrified it may not be true. Like her, Beatrice turns savagely on her lover:

> *Benedick.* You take pleasure then in the message[3]
> *Beatrice.* Yea, just so much as you may take upon a knife's point.
> (II.iii. 241–2)

[3] *message* – i.e., to come in for dinner.

36 Beatrice (Judi Dench) and Hero's waiting women prepare Hero (Cherie Lunghi) for her ill-fated marriage ceremony, 1976

The turning point for Beatrice comes when she is the intended eaves-dropper to the conversation about herself and Benedick that has been dreamed up by Hero and Ursula. Their words are 'fire' in her ears, for Hero has touched a sensitive nerve by accusing Beatrice of pride and disdain. In her soliloquy, Beatrice promises:

> If thou dost love, my kindness shall incite thee
> To bind our loves up in a holy band.
>   (III.i. 113–14)

Such a reaction would be impossible were she not already in love with him. Otherwise she could use the information as capital from which to create more jokes at Benedick's expense. It is likewise yet another proof of her unwillingness to come to terms with her own feelings that she puts the burden of success or failure of their relationship onto Benedick: 'if *thou* dost love . . .' In each of the scenes in which the two of them seriously discuss their feelings (IV.i. and V.iv.), Beatrice is unwilling to commit herself—until she is certain that Benedick means what he says. Although the second of these concludes with the dance that ends the play on a happy, harmonious note, the pairing of the two 'witcrackers' leaves a number of questions unanswered. The most significant of these regards their knowledge of each other's feelings. We can tell, because we have the advantage of all-seeing eyes, that they love each other, but they have never confessed it unequivocally face to face. It is only by kissing her that Benedick silences Beatrice and stops her from going on yet another steeple chase of puns and jokes in response to his proposal of marriage.

Even at the last she cannot forsake the habit of covering up her true feelings. Marriage has always provoked ambiguous reactions from her for although she affects to despise it (II.i. 62–9), Hero's betrothal clearly reminds her sharply of her own single state: 'I may sit in a corner and cry heigh-ho for a husband!' Her speeches are virtually all concerned either with marriage or with Benedick. The fact that she chooses for the most part to despise both is neither here nor there: the point is that these matters were preying on her mind. She is in love with Benedick and wants to marry him, but this is revealed only indirectly for she is too proud and fearful to scrutinise her emotions accurately. Shakespeare's portrait of her is masterly because he lets us discover her as we would a person in real life, without any kind of intrusive explanation. Neither does he 'resolve' her problem, for as indicated above, the trait of instinctive self-defence through wit is with her to the last.

The underlying tensions and the gentle probing into motive that characterise *Much Ado About Nothing*, are not to be found in *As You Like It*. Another marked difference is that here there are very definitely two heroines, not a heroine and her pale foil. Rosalind has been the close friend of Celia from their earliest years, but unlike Hermia and Helena of *A Midsummer Night's Dream*, whose friendship comes closest to theirs, they are not divided by jealousy over men. By the end of the play each has met, and been paired off with, the husband she desires, but it is not at the expense of her affection for the other. In this play, Shakespeare shows that more than one strong feeling can be sustained at once: being in love with one person does not preclude loving another.

From the outset the close bond between Celia and Rosalind is emphasised. Rosalind's father has been banished by Duke Frederick who has allowed her to stay in his court as company for his daughter Celia. To comfort Rosalind, Celia promises to return the wealth and land that have been taken from her father, as soon as Duke Frederick dies: 'and when I break that oath, let me turn monster. Therefore, my sweet Rose, my dear Rose, be merry.' Her motives spring entirely from her warm nature. When her father banishes Rosalind because he fears her popularity with his subjects, Celia speaks of the long time they have known each other. At first:

> I was too young that time to value her;
> But now I know her: if she be a traitor,
> Why so am I; we still have slept together,[4]
> Rose at an instant, learn'd, play'd, eat together;
> And whereso'er we went, like Juno's swans,
> Still we went coupled and inseparable.
>
> (I.iii. 67–72)

Such dedicated loyalty between women is not found elsewhere in Shakespeare, except between mistress and servant, where it cannot be equally balanced. Celia and Rosalind are 'coupled and inseparable'. Celia is willing to defy her father in order to support her friend, and when Rosalind cannot believe that Celia will leave with her, her friend gently rebukes her:

---

[4] *slept together*: not in a sexual sense. Although jokes about, and references to, homosexuality between men are to be found in Shakespeare, there is no equivalent for women. Like Beatrice's remark in *Much Ado* (IV.i. 149–51), Celia is here referring to the Elizabethan habit of allowing members of the same sex to share the same bed.

37 Julia Neilson as a robust Rosalind in an 1896 production of *As You Like It*

> Rosalind lacks then the love
> Which teacheth thee that thou and I am one:
> Shall we be sunder'd? shall we part, sweet girl?
> No: let my father seek another heir.
>
> (I.iii. 92–5)

At this stage Celia is shown as the leader, the one who makes plans and acts on decisions. She supports Rosalind, who frequently needs comforting. There is a subtle change as soon as Rosalind adopts her disguise as a boy, for as she says:

> in my heart
> Lie there what hidden woman's fear there will
> We'll have a swashing and a martial outside.
>
> (I.iii. 114–16)

Her outward appearance as a man gives her both confidence and courage. When she and Celia come to the Forest of Arden, she is the comforter when they are tired and a little frightened, for she adopts the man's role: 'doublet and hose ought to show itself courageous to petticoat.' Similarly, she is now the one who makes arrangements for their new life-style in the Forest, by buying a cottage and a flock of sheep (II.iv. 89–101). Although there is no suggestion that affection between them diminishes, from this point Rosalind commands more of the audience's attention than Celia, and she is shown as more resourceful and robust than her friend.

Partly this is because of the plot. When they arrive in the Forest, Rosalind is already in love with Orlando, now banished like her, but Celia has no one. It is, incidentally, further proof of Celia's selfless loyalty that there is not an ounce of jealousy in her. She professes to love Orlando for her friend's sake and apart from teasing her a little when Rosalind is desperate for news of him, does everything she can to bring them together. She does not play gooseberry for long, however, because she falls in love with Oliver, the once-wicked but now reformed elder brother of Orlando. Their courtship is non-existent from the audience's point of view, but we are told within two scenes of their meeting that: 'They are in the very wrath of love, and they will together: clubs cannot part them.' Celia's destiny is rapidly worked out in this way because by Act V the interest is firmly centred on Rosalind, whose disguise has provoked a number of curious situations.

38 Touchstone's crude courtship of Audrey contrasts with the idyllic relationships envisaged for Celia and Rosalind. Courtice Pounds as Touchstone and Marianne Cauldwell as Audrey, 1907

Like Julia in *The Two Gentlemen of Verona* her wearing of boy's clothes has enabled her to get close to her lover and find out the truth of his feelings for her. Rosalind does not become his page, but proposes a more complicated relationship, which involves a deception-within-a-deception.

What she suggests is that Orlando 'cures' himself of his love by coming to her cottage every day to woo her, giving her the name of Rosalind. The situation that emerges is fraught with irony and ambiguity: Rosalind, assuming the personality of a youth, Ganymede, is wooed by her real lover, who calls her Rosalind while believing she is a boy! The choice of the name Ganymede[5] provides a homosexual joke to add to the general confusion of identities, and an additionally discordant element is added when a shepherdess, Phebe, falls in love with the disguised Rosalind. The plot is as swift-moving as a situational comedy like *The Comedy of Errors*, but the tone is lighter, funnier and, apart from being assured of a happy ending, we are unable to predict what will happen from moment to moment. It is also one of Shakespeare's more ambitious plots: the parallel loves of Celia and Oliver, Rosalind and Orlando, are contrasted not only with that of the idealised pastoral figures of Phebe and Silvius, but also the amorous cavortings of the sluttish goat-girl Audrey and the court jester Touchstone. When Rosalind puts on her woman's clothes once more she retains the independent spirit she assumed in disguise, for she is the voice of order prevailing over chaos. By the end of Act V she is the only character with the knowledge necessary to unravel all the tangled relationships that bewilder her companions and she dominates the final scene in the play, pairing off all the couples, including herself and Orlando. From being a fearful refugee in the Forest of Arden, she has changed into a self-possessed young woman whose opinions are sought and respected. The light-heartedness, wit and intelligence are still there, but she has become more thoughtfully aware of others than before. Her character-development far outstrips her cousin's, for Celia remains essentially the same after her arrival in the forest. There is no doubt that Rosalind's sudden maturity is initiated by her role-playing as a boy, for she has the chance of a type of freedom and command that is denied to Celia.

Disguise also leads to greater self-confidence and profounder understanding in *Twelfth Night*, but here it is taken on early in Act I. We see

[5] *Ganymede*: youthful lover of Zeus, as well as being his cup-bearer.

very little of Viola (who disguises herself as the page Caesario) when she is in woman's clothes, and so the ambivalence and fascination of her character is extended over virtually the full five acts.

The play has, as part of its plot, a more sophisticated version of the lost twins seen in *The Comedy of Errors*. More scope is allowed too, because the twins are of different sexes. Viola fears that her twin, Sebastian, may have been drowned in the shipwreck that separated them but hopes for the best and sets about dealing with present problems. These traits of optimism and realism set her in contrast with the dreamy, self-centred Olivia. She too has lost a brother, but wants to nurture the sorrow of his death by refusing to go out for seven years, constantly wearing a veil and weeping once a day. The setting of such a rigid code is at variance with nature, a self-delusion that is reminiscent of Navarre's ruling that no man in his court should see a woman for three years (*Love's Labour's Lost*). There is a strongly self-indulgent streak in Olivia, for she can forget the strictures she herself has imposed as soon as the attractive Caesario appears. Her curiosity is aroused when she sees him, and she is so taken with his wit and appearance that she removes her veil in the hope of making him fall in love with her. The irony that Caesario is really Viola has particular sharpness since that lady, like Julia before her in *Two Gentlemen of Verona*, is wooing her on behalf of the man with whom she is herself in love. By contrast with Olivia's sentimental attachment to Caesario, Viola's love for Orsino is almost painfully real.

We have no revelation of how she fell in love with Duke Orsino, for she entered his service as a page with little knowledge of him. She confesses her love in an aside with no preliminaries, when he has sent her to court Olivia on his behalf: 'Whoe'er I woo, myself would be his wife.' When her wooing is so successful that Olivia falls in love with her, instead of looking more kindly on Orsino, Viola's soliloquy reveals the dilemma brought about by her disguise:

What will become of this? As I am man,
My state is desperate[6] for my master's love;
As I am woman—now alas the day!—
What thriftless sighs shall poor Olivia breathe!
(II.ii. 35–8)

She is sensitive to the feelings of all concerned, and her compassion excites our sympathy for her own case. Nowhere is she more clearly the

[6] *desperate*: impossible.

victim of her disguise than when Orsino speaks of his infatuation with Olivia. He boasts:

> There is no woman's sides
> Can bide the beating of so strong a passion
> As love doth give my heart.
>
> (II.iv. 94–6)

His belittling of what women feel nearly forces Viola to reveal herself as a living contradiction to his words, but she stops herself and compromises by assigning her feelings to a mythical sister who:

> never told her love,
> But let concealment, like a worm i' the bud,
> Feed on her damask cheek: she pin'd in thought,
> And with a green and yellow melancholy,
> She sat like Patience on a monument,
> Smiling at grief.
>
> (II.iv. 111–16)

The lines are justly famous. Viola, even as she speaks, exemplifies the image of Patience, inwardly suffering, outwardly smiling, unable to do anything but wait. There is a temptation for an instant to feel Viola's situation as a tragedy, but Shakespeare rescues us by not allowing further introspection. Within a few more lines the scene and tone changes with the entrance of the buffoon, Sir Toby Belch and his sottish friends. We are not allowed to dwell on Viola's sorrows. A dangerous moment has been averted.

Peril for Viola herself almost occurs when she is challenged to a duel with Sir Andrew Aguecheek, a foolish and unsuccessful suitor of Olivia's. They have actually drawn swords when Sebastian's friend Antonio rushes in to separate them. No other Shakespearian heroine who uses disguise is put to so many tests to delight the audience and, on a more serious level, to see if she can keep up her appearance. Viola passes them all, with the result that we admire her loyalty to Orsino, her respect for Olivia and her courage in the face of a range of vicissitudes. The joyful reunion between Viola and Sebastian comes as the reward for her sufferings, for now she can throw away her 'masculine usurp'd attire' and confront Orsino with the truth. Humbled by her devotion to him, his earlier pose of languor and a taste for exaggerated compliments drop from Orsino like Viola's cast-off clothing. They face each other stripped of delusion and disguise when he proposes to her.

118

And some have greatness thrust upon them.

39 Malvolio tricked into wearing 'yellow stockings cross-gartered' and perpetually smiling in the hope of winning Olivia in *Twelfth Night*. Rose le Clerq as Olivia and Henry Irving as Malvolio in 1884

Olivia, like Orsino, is shown as in love with the *idea* of love, and in a sense, Viola is the agent of her release from self-indulgence. Olivia falls in love with the image presented by Caesario, and transposes this affection completely on to Sebastian, both before and after she realises that he is not Orsino's page. Olivia's character is, however, less accessible to us than Viola's, partly for the structural reason that there are fewer opportunities for her to reveal different facets of her personality. This is not to say that she is a cardboard figure. The conversations with those in her household are spiced with humour and good sense—it is only with regard to her own motives and actions that she is obtuse. When Viola, in the guise of Caesario, lavishes praise on her, culminating in the claim that she would be cruel to die unmarried and childless, leaving the world with no copy of her beauty, Olivia shows amused detachment in her reply:

> O! Sir, I will not be so hard-hearted; I will give out divers schedules of my beauty: it shall be inventoried, and every particle and utensil labelled to my will: as *Item*, Two lips, indifferent red; *Item*, Two grey eyes, with lids to them; *Item*, One neck, one chin, and so forth.

> (I.v. 247–52)

Much of the witty patter in the play comes from neither Viola nor Olivia, but from Olivia's forceful serving-woman, Maria. She is cast in the same mould as Juliet's nurse, a good-hearted busy-body. She bustles around Olivia's house, scolding Sir Toby for his drunkenness one minute and planning a trick on the love-sick steward Malvolio the next. Her lively presence adds greatly to the richness and variety of tone in the play, for her down-to-earth humour contrasts with the extravagant language of her social superiors.

In moving to what are often termed the 'last' or 'problem' plays, we encounter a group unified by one outstanding feature. *Pericles, Cymbeline, The Winter's Tale* and *The Tempest* are all concerned in some way with a father's loss of his child or children and their subsequent reunion. Divisions are healed and the reunions herald a new era of peace and prosperity. There are obvious similarities between this structure and tragedy, but only the unrepentantly evil are killed[7] and there is a predominant theme of forgiveness in the Last Plays, and so they are here annexed to the Comedies.

Pericles is the least known of the four. Because of the unevenness of poetry and characterisation, it is still thought by some scholars to be not entirely the work of Shakespeare. It chronicles the adventures of Pericles, Prince of Tyre, with every act introduced to us by the figure of the medieval poet John Gower. This cumbersome device interrupts the flow of the plot, but does help to clarify the action which takes place in six different localities. The following is a brief outline of the plot:

Pericles first sets out for Antioch, as a suitor for the hand of the king's

---

[7] With the exception of Antigonus in *The Winter's Tale*.

daughter. In true fairy-tale fashion, he has to solve a riddle before he can win her. He does so, but here the fairy story ends. The king has concealed in the riddle the truth of his relationship with his daughter and Pericles finds him out: the two have been living together incestuously. Pericles wisely leaves the island in haste, for the king is out to kill him. After various other journeys, he is shipwrecked at Pentapolis. In spite of having only rusty, salt-stained armour to wear, Pericles so distinguishes himself in a tournament to celebrate the king's daughter's birthday that she falls in love with him and they are married. Eventually he sails back to Tyre with her but Thaisa is so terrified by a fierce storm that she gives premature birth to their daughter and is thought dead. She is buried at sea, but her coffin floats to Ephesus where she is revived. Out of fidelity to her husband, whom she is sure she will never see again, Thaisa becomes high priestess at the temple of Diana. In the meantime, Pericles, certain that his baby Marina will die before they reach Tyre, leaves her in the care of friends in Tarsus. Marina grows up in the Governor's family, but his wife Dionyza becomes so jealous of her beauty and talents, which eclipse those of her own daughter, that she arranges to have Marina murdered. The girl is 'rescued' by pirates, who later sell her to the owner of a brothel. Here her virtue is such that she reforms every man who tries to take her virginity, proving such bad business for the brothel that the owners let her go to an 'honest' house where she becomes famous for her singing and dancing. Pericles chances to visit the place and the two are reunited. He has a vision from the Goddess Diana instructing him to visit her temple and there he finds his wife. Thaisa's father is now dead and so Pericles and his wife return as rulers of his kingdom. Marina marries a man she reformed while in the brothel, and they are made rulers of Tyre.

On one level the play concerns appearance and reality as exemplified by the contrasting sets of characters. Among the women there is evil which appears evil (the Bawd in the brothel), good which appears good (Thaisa and Marina), and evil which appears good (the incestuous daughter, whom Pericles aptly terms a 'glorious casket stor'd with ill,' and Dionyza). There is an unusually overt moral tone for Shakespeare, as human frailty is exposed: the good do not recognise evil if it is well-enough disguised. Justice will ultimately be meted out by some higher power, as the reward of virtue, and this is proved in the play for all the villains die, whereas the good, despite trials and suffering, prosper. Gower's final words make the point, although we could hardly have missed it, that we have:

40 Pericles is reunited with his wife, Thaisa, who has become a priestess in the temple of Diana. From the Regent's Park production in 1939

In Pericles, his queen, and daughter, seen—
Although assail'd with fortune fierce and keen—
Virtue preserv'd from fell destruction's blast,
Led on by heaven, and crown'd with joy at last.
(V.iii. 87–90)

On this carousel of black-and-white characters, Marina is the only one apart from Pericles to have any colour in her personality. She is shown as an agent of redemption through virtue, a factor that links her with the heroines of *All's Well* and *Measure for Measure*, although she is more touching than either Helena or Isabella. We meet her looking for flowers to put on her old nurse's grave. She plucks them with such tender concern that when the scheming Dionyza deceives her into parting with the bunch, 'ere the sea mar it' (IV.i. 26), Marina's compliance causes particularly sharp anguish. It is the same innocent trust that nearly results in her death; the flowers she puts into Dionyza's hands are a symbol of Marina's own life. Alone with the man whom Dionyza has ordered to murder her, Marina cannot understand what fault she has committed:

I never did her hurt in all my life.
I never spake bad word, nor did ill turn
To any living creature; believe me—
I never killed a mouse, nor hurt a fly.
I trod upon a worm against my will,
But I wept for it.
(IV.i. 75–80)

The catalogue of virtues is saved from sounding unconvincing by the simple diction and the poignant interjection 'believe me'. Her gentle nature is utterly credible. Further proof lies in her method of reforming the men who hope to use her as a prostitute. She appeals to the qualities in their natures that are so evident in hers: honour and plain-speaking, tempered with gentleness. Her success also suggests a more profound message: anyone may be redeemed, no matter how gross his self-indulgence.

The heroine of *Cymbeline*, Imogen, is also a sensitive creature, but she lacks the ethereal quality so evident in Marina. Her sublime courage in the face of terrible odds is very much on a human level, for she withstands them suffering and alone. The combination of her tender-

123

hearted innocence and active, but for the most part solitary, moral virtue, makes her one of the most compelling of Shakespeare's women. Perhaps it was this that moved Swinburne to call her 'the woman best beloved in . . . all the tide of time'.[8]

Her husband has been banished, and her waiting-woman has barely two lines, so Imogen has no lover or confidante to help her. It is this isolation from any kind or guiding influence that gives us such a sharp sense of concern for her, right from the first scene of the play. Consequently, her reunion with husband, father and brothers brings a sense of unusual relief.

Imogen's exceptional beauty is brought to our notice obliquely, by remarks made by gentlemen at her father's court, and by the villainous Iachimo as he gazes at her when she is asleep. He is so entranced by her loveliness as to exclaim:

> 'Tis her breathing that
> Perfumes the chamber thus; the flame of the taper
> Bows toward her, and would under-peep her lids,
> To see the enclosed lights now canopied
> Under these windows, white and azure lac'd
> With blue of heaven's own tint.
>
> (II.ii. 18–23)

The delicate image to describe her eyes has considerable impact coming as it does from Iachimo, who has earlier been shown capable of only mouthing lewd jokes and lascivious sneers. But Imogen is far more than outwardly beautiful.

Iachimo deceives the banished Posthumus, Imogen's husband, into thinking that she is unchaste. Posthumus in fury sends a message to his old servant Pisanio, ordering him to kill Imogen, but Pisanio cannot bring himself to murder a creature 'more goddess-like than wife-like'. When Imogen learns what Posthumus has demanded, her reaction is not fear or self-pity but cold fury, for she thinks her husband has found another woman:

> I am stale, a garment out of fashion,
> And, for I am richer than to hang by the walls,
> I must be ripp'd; to pieces with me! O!
> Men's vows are women's traitors!
>
> (III.iv. 53–6)

[8] *A Study of Shakespeare*, 1880.

124

There is no simpering romanticism here: Imogen's savage words, ('I must be *ripp'd*) show an ability to look death and the horrors of death, full in the face. Indeed, the sense of her own honour is so absolute that she would rather die than be thought false. She begs the by now horrified Pisanio to kill her: 'The lamb entreats the butcher: where's thy knife?' No other woman in Shakespeare is given this dimension of extraordinary physical courage. Even Cleopatra, seizing death triumphantly, does not betray the realisation that dying may be violent and painful. (And it is not, for her.) Imogen thinks otherwise, as reflected by the violent images she uses, and her courage is the greater because her sense of virtuous conduct overwhelms her fear. Another occasion exemplifies her bravery. Disguised as a boy in order to look for Posthumus, she loses her way in the Welsh hills but finds an obviously inhabited cave. Fear momentarily overcomes her:

> I were best not call, I dare not call, yet famine,
> E'er clean it o'er throw nature, makes it valiant.
> (III.vi. 19–20)

Made bold by hunger she draws her sword and calls, 'Ho! Who's here?' into the mouth of the cave. The point is not that the pangs of hunger were greater than her terror of the unknown, but that, for whatever reason, she is able to tread down her fear.

A further quality that makes Imogen seem more in control and more mature than other heroines in the Comedies and Last Plays in her clear-sightedness. When we first meet her, she is in the company of the Queen and her comment, as that woman leaves, sums up her cunning, deceitful nature in an instant:

> Dissembling courtesy. How fine this tyrant
> Can tickle where she wounds!
> (I.i. 84–5)

She also sees through Iachimo's lies about her husband's infidelity the moment he says he wants to sleep with her:

> Away! I do condemn mine ears that have
> So long attended thee. If thou wert honourable,
> Thou wouldst have told this tale for virtue, not
> For such an end thou seek'st.
> (I.vi. 141–4)

41 A dramatic sketch of Henry Irving in 1896 as Iachimo creeping out of the trunk in Imogen's bedchamber. Imogen is played by Ellen Terry

The only way that Iachimo can deceive her is while she lies asleep, and in this her trust and integrity are shown as somewhat greater than Posthumus', who was taken in completely by Iachimo's 'proofs' of Imogen's lust.

In addition to these rather stern virtues, Imogen is shown capable of a considerable range of expression and feeling. At one extreme, there is the kind of plain, almost homely language, most moving in the scene in which she believes that she is burying her husband's headless corpse but, still disguised as a page, tells a Roman Captain that it is her master's body. She agrees to follow the Captain,

> But first, an't please the gods,
> I'll hide my master from the flies, as deep
> As these poor pickaxes can dig.
> (IV.ii. 387–9)

The restraint and simplicity of the language convey her grief and the harsh conditions of the burial with painful accuracy. It is hard to read, 'I'll hide my master from the flies,' without a shudder: the words force us to think of the corpse as rotting meat, the headless, bleeding trunk attracting blowflies. The pathetic 'my master' is ambiguous, reminding us that Imogen believes she is burying her husband's body but dare not reveal his, or her own, identity to the Captain.

At the other extreme, Imogen can speak in intricate metaphors, as when she imagines how she would have watched Posthumus sail away:

> I would have broke mine eye-strings, crack'd them, but
> To look upon him, till the diminution
> Of space had pointed him sharp as my needle,
> Nay, follow'd him, till he had melted from
> The smallness of a gnat to air, and then
> Have turn'd mine eye, and wept.
> (I.iii. 17–22)

Such delicate mingling of the intellectual concept and sensitive imagery would be arresting in its own right, but is particularly so in *Cymbeline*, where much of the language is, by contrast, coarse and brutal. (A good example is Cloten's description of a lute, after the lovely song 'Hark! Hark! the lark', as 'horse-hairs and calves' guts' (II.iii. 32–3).)

The character of Imogen therefore emerges as complex as any woman in Shakespeare. Although she bears a similarity to some of the earlier comic heroines (notably Portia, because of her wisdom), she seems older

127

than they are, her sensibility shaped by suffering. However, there is an elusive quality about her, perhaps because her significance recedes in the final act, which is largely given over to the rather tedious unravelling of Cymbeline's family and political tangles. It says a great deal for the force and subtlety of her portrait in the earlier acts that our feeling for her is sustained to the end, and that her reunion with Cymbeline and her husband is the supreme moment of the last scene.

The Winter's Tale also concerns the theme of a loving and dutiful wife wrongly accused of adultery, but Hermione shows nothing of Imogen's righteous anger. She is immediately prepared to excuse her husband:

> Should a villain say so,
> The most replenish'd villain in the world
> He were as much more villain: you, my lord,
> Do but mistake.
>
> (II.i. 78–81)

She admits that she is 'not prone to weeping' but that she has:

> That honourable grief lodg'd here which burns
> Worse than tears drown.
>
> (II.i. 111–12)

In spite of such explanations, her words never seem to bring us close to her suffering; she has no soliloquies and remains just out of our reach, a remote and passionless figure. The cadences of her long speeches contesting Leontes' indictment are eloquent and measured, but their very logic and polish encourages us to approach Hermione intellectually rather than through the language of the heart. We can compare Imogen's request, made almost peremptory through tension and fierce emotion— 'The lamb entreats the butcher: where's thy knife?'—with Hermione's much cooler and more reflective words to Leontes:

> To me can life be no commodity:
> The crown and comfort of my life, your favour,
> I do give lost; for I do feel it gone,
> And know not how it went.
>
> (III.ii. 93–6)

Both are wronged women, begging for death rather than a life in

128

ignominy, but Hermione is able to withdraw into objective comment. Her personality is essentially an image of perfect fidelity, made visual for us, by Shakespeare's masterstroke in Act V when she is revealed as the 'living statue'.

Warmer life pulses through the veins of her daughter, Perdita. Leontes rejected her at birth, ordering one of his lords, Antigonus, to leave the baby in some deserted place, otherwise, Leontes claimed savagely:

> The bastard brains with these my proper hands
> Shall I dash out.
>
> (II.iii. 139–40)

Although Antigonus meets a grisly death (his final exit is described in Shakespeare's most famous stage-direction: *pursued by a bear*), the child is found and adopted by shepherds. Our first sight of her is sixteen years later, and the love-match between her and young Florizel intensifies our awareness of the new life-force that will return to the now-penitent Leontes, once his daughter is found. Her language sparkles with energy and colour, reflecting her close association with nature. Here she longs for spring flowers to give Florizel:

> daffodils,
> That come before the swallow dares, and take
> The winds of March with beauty; violets dim
> ... pale primroses
> That die unmarried ...
>
> (IV.iv. 118–22)

There is a freshness and warm innocence about her relationship with Florizel, shown in playful sexuality when he teases her that she wants to cover him up with flowers like a corpse: 'No, like a bank for love to lie and play on' she laughingly replies. She wants him very much alive and 'in mine arms'.

The final reunion with her father and his reconciliation with Polixenes take place off-stage, thus avoiding the sort of tedium the audience had to suffer in Act V of *Cymbeline*, and allowing full focus on the unveiling of Hermione. Perdita steps out of the spotlight, but first we see sufficient of her meeting with Leontes to mark how dramatically her beauty and natural dignity affect him, even before he knows who she is. She begins the thaw that is complete at the moment when Leontes takes Hermione in his arms and joyously exclaims: 'O! She's warm!' (V.iii.

109). The chill of death and winter that has been so long present at Leontes' court is at last ended.

Before leaving the play, mention must be made of Paulina, Antigonus' wife and a lady at Leontes' court. Her case is almost unique in Shakespeare because although her own interests are of very little consequence and subordinated in every way to those of Hermione and Perdita, her character has a roundness and potency that far exceeds theirs. The only possible parallel to her would be Mistress Quickly.[9]

Her function in the play is primarily to act as the voice of truth and reason to Leontes. She forces her way into his court with the newly-born Perdita, for as she has said earlier:

> We do not know
> How he may soften at the sight of the child.
> (II.ii. 39–40)

Leontes' reaction is ferocious, but Paulina withstands his fury, and, unlike the men in his court, is not afraid to speak her mind. Leontes even threatens to burn her, but she retorts:

> I care not:
> It is an heretic that makes the fire,
> Not she which burns in it.
> (II.iii. 114–16)

Since she is voicing our own feelings about Leontes, our sympathies are totally with her, so we can exult in the courage and dignity she displays as she leaves. Leontes has peremptorily told her to get out, and Paulina's frostily courteous response reflects her sublime sang-froid: 'I pray you do not push me; I'll be gone.'

When Leontes refuses even to believe the words of the Oracle that Hermione is chaste, and she falls, apparently dead from shock and sorrow, it is Paulina who berates the king. When she learns that he has at last repented, her own forgiveness and compassion are immediate. She blames herself for speaking so harshly when he is already mortified at his own stupidity:

> Alas! I have show'd too much
> The rashness of a woman: he is touch'd
> To the noble heart. What's gone and what's past help
> Should be past grief: do not receive affliction
> At my petition.
> (III.ii. 220–4)

---

[9] *Mistress Quickly*: hostess of the Boar's Head Tavern, appears in *Henry IV*, Part 1, *Henry IV*, Part 2 and *Henry V*.

The game of love is present in all the Comedies and Last Plays. Sometimes it is almost hidden, as in *Cymbeline*, where one player wrongly accuses another of breaking the rules and there are many terrible moments before the game can be resumed. Occasionally people play it without even realising that they have begun to make the moves, like Beatrice in *Much Ado*. Most often there are two or three different games going on at the same time, but the players, for a gamut of reasons, are unable to settle into balanced partnerships until the end. In some measure each of these love-games is a game of chess, the symbol suggested for Miranda and Ferdinand. We cannot help but notice that Shakespeare is paying an indirect tribute to the importance of women, for in chess the most versatile, powerful and treasured piece is the queen.

IV

Women in the Histories

Alas, poor wenches, where are now your fortunes?

Henry VII III.i. 148

Lightheartedness and game-playing are almost entirely absent from
Shakespeare's History Plays. Here the women achieve importance not
so much for subtle facets of their behaviour and personalities but
because they are immediately recognisable as representatives of a particular 'type'. Female figures of this kind are also found in certain other
plays, such as *Coriolanus* and *Troilus and Cressida* and are therefore included for discussion in this chapter with the 'historical' women.
Another link is that all of these plays, like the Histories, are predomin-
antly concerned with male authority. Whether weak, holy, foolish or
strong, it is the men whose use and abuse of power shape the destinies of
the other characters. Women are significant only in as far as they explain
some aspect of a hero's character. Usually this is by their direct
influence, as in the case of Volumnia, Coriolanus' archetypally possessive mother.

Obviously there are similarities between such women and the
heroines in the tragedies. Both are secondary in importance to the men
but used to show up telling characteristics in them. The women in the
Histories and allied plays are, however, less complex, more predictable
and usually have their significant moments confined to one part of the
play and sometimes to only one scene. A Cleopatra, a Juliet or a Cordelia
makes far greater demands on our hearts and minds because her fate and
character are more vital to the unfolding of the plot. Even if, as in Cordelia's case, a woman destined for a tragic end makes only brief
appearances, other characters talk of her in her absence and keep her in
our thoughts. It is an important aspect of Shakespeare's genius that in
the Histories and other plays where our interest is steered away from the
individual, personal fates of the women, he rarely allows them to appear
simply as two-dimensional stereotypes.

In the interesting group of women who represent moral laxity

44 There are only two women in *Timon of Athens*, and both are whores. In this Czechoslo-vakian production they are trapped together in a net, perhaps to suggest that they are imprisoned by their loose living, 1969

through varying degrees of sexual indulgence, it is only the two mistresses of Alcibiades in *Timon of Athens* who are utterly forgettable through being so lightly sketched. Alcibiades is the foil to Timon, for they have both been unjustly rejected by society, but Alcibiades is able to compromise, unlike his bitter counterpart. It is significant that there are no women in the play apart from Alcibiades' 'brace of harlots', used only for their bodies. The atmosphere surrounding Timon is one of unalleviated cynicism and despair with no love-interest to pierce the gloom. The mistresses disgust him and he addresses one of them with a familiarity that suggests his revulsion springs from personal recollection:

Art thou Timandra?
. . .
Be a whore still; they love thee not that use thee;
Give them diseases, leaving with thee their lust.
(IV.iii. 81–4)

The two soon depart with Alcibiades and do not reappear. They have fulfilled their purpose in the drama, which is to stress the fact that Timon's miseries are exacerbated by having no women in his life, not even a prostitute. The thought of sexual pleasure nauseates him and the appearance of Timandra and her companion brings to the surface his hatred of women. His misanthropy is total. He wishes Alcibiades well in his proposed attack on Athens and with chill savagery imagines the slaughter of old men, mothers and babies. All are deceitful and corrupt in his eyes, even the young girl, because her:

> milk-paps
> That through the window-bars bore at men's eyes,
> Are not within the leaf of pity writ,
> But . . . horrible traitors.
>
> (IV.iii. 114–17)

Alcibiades' two whores therefore allow us to glimpse an important facet of Timon's tragedy, even though they are insignificant characters themselves.

Shakespeare's most ebullient and famous lady of easy virtue, Mistress Nell Quickly, is certainly not insignificant. She appears in *Henry IV*, Parts 1 and 2, and *Henry V*, where her continued presence helps to link the three plays. She is mistress of the Boar's Head Tavern, sited in the seedy and unfashionable district of Eastcheap. Nell, her tavern and her customers represent London's low-life, a far cry from Westminster Palace where Henry IV holds court, but a haven for one particularly irresponsible and renegade member of the aristocracy, Sir John Falstaff. Prince Hal, the future King Henry V, is Falstaff's protégé in loose-living until he becomes monarch, cursing, carousing, whoring and generally abnegating all sense of sober responsibility. Since one of the key issues in the two parts of *Henry IV* is whether Hal will make a good king and restore order to England despite the dissipations of his youth as Prince of Wales, Mistress Quickly's establishment and the attractions it offers are of great importance. Falstaff invariably succumbs to such temptations when he should be elsewhere, but until the end of *Henry IV*, Part 2, we cannot be sure that Hal will not follow in his footsteps. The style and quality of life pursued by Mistress Quickly and the whore Doll Tearsheet who works in her tavern therefore form not only the context for spotlighting the character of Falstaff, but also have a direct bearing on

45 Mistress Quickly, played by Elizabeth Spriggs, and a group of ale-swillers in the Boar's Head Tavern, 1966

the fortunes of the Prince. Ultimately he must choose between this kind of lazy, self-indulgent life, and the sterner demands of discipline and duty. When the moment comes he rejects Falstaff with the words that cut him to the heart:

> I know thee not, old man: fall to thy prayers,
> How ill white hairs become a fool and jester,
> (V.v. 47–8)

It is significant that Nell and Doll have just been marched off by the Beadles. It is as though every trace of Henry V's youthful follies has been swept away, heralding a new, strong regime. Nell appears again in *Henry V*, but only briefly. Now that the king is clearly established as a man of integrity, the seamy side of life and the diversions it offers no longer pose a threat to the well-being of the nation, for Henry has turned resolutely away from them. Falstaff, too, no longer has the chance to exert an evil influence over Henry, and he does not appear on stage. We hear that he has died, fittingly enough, in Nell Quickly's tavern, for: 'The king has killed his heart.' Mistress Quickly's function in this play is perhaps to show that whether good or bad reigns at the top, there will always be a demand for the sort of services she offers. The pattern of life she, Doll Tearsheet and the frequenters of her tavern enjoy, continues undisturbed and relatively unaffected by civil war, prosperity or peace. Shakespeare suggests to the audience that human nature is such that the treacherous undertow pulling men and women down to drunkenness, promiscuity and brawling is an inescapable aspect of society. It is only in the Histories that he gives this searching look into the murky waters of London's side-streets because part of his purpose in these plays is to reveal society at large.

As a key figure in the lower reaches, Nell Quickly ultimately emerges with a spirited and individual character that effectively transcends her symbolic function.

The first part of *Henry IV* is much concerned with the pranks of Prince Hal and Falstaff, and the Boar's Head provides the setting for jocular and frequently coarse verbal scuffles between the two. At first Mistress Quickly is notable only for a tendency to preface every remark with, 'O Jesu!' and a simple-minded admiration of Falstaff. A more fiery side to her character is shown in Act III, her final appearance in the play, when Falstaff accuses her of being party to stealing from him. The sparring between them demonstrates Nell's gift for saucy repartee but also shows how gullible she really is. Falstaff has only to say to her:

> Hostess, I forgive thee ... thou shalt find me tractable to any honest reason: thou seest I am pacified.

> (III.iii. 170–3)

and even though she is the one who should be forgiving him she is immediately won over and prepared to forget how he has insulted her. It is a pattern repeated more elaborately in *Henry IV*, Part 2, in which both Nell and Doll are shown to be completely under Falstaff's thumb. Here Nell has gone as far as suing him for debt but when challenged as to the amount it is clear that it is not the money that is at the root of her complaint, but that Falstaff has not kept his word in another way:

> Thou didst swear to me ... to marry me and make me my lady thy wife. Canst thou deny it?

> (II.i. 89–91)

Her pain at his broken vows is shown in her frantic insistence on irrelevant details of their last meeting as if to force truth into his words by recalling the circumstances under which they were spoken:

> Did not goodwife Keech, the butcher's wife, come in then and call me gossip Quickly? Coming in to borrow a mess of vinegar; telling us she had a good dish of prawns...
>
> (II.i. 91–4)

Such prattle has the obvious comic purpose of showing how Nell is her own worst enemy, but at times there also comes a curious note of pathos, out of key with the rest. The two tones are evident in her plangent accusation: 'And didst thou not kiss me and bid me fetch thee thirty shillings?' The recollection of Falstaff's kiss is on the verge of a tenderness and vulnerability that Mistress Quickly is far too much a hardened woman of the world ever to admit. Accordingly it is immediately followed by the sharply contrasting memory of how Falstaff used the occasion to wheedle money out of her. For a moment we had been in peril of taking Nell Quickly too seriously and losing sight of the real interest of the scene, which is Falstaff's reaction to her threats. By haranging him once again about money rather than the more subtle and dangerous matters of the heart, Nell brings us back to safe ground. Falstaff can now confidently take over the scene, charming Nell into withdrawing her charge and lending him even more money. At the beginning of the scene she has screamed abuse at him, calling him 'bastardly rogue', 'honey-suckle villain' and 'hempseed', but as soon as he has placated her with false promises it becomes, 'Prithee, Sir John . . .'. She even offers him the whore Doll for the evening. All of this happens rather too quickly for us to feel that Nell is making a genuinely painful sacrifice but we are certainly aware of Falstaff's extraordinary hold over her. The same is true in his relationship with Doll Tearsheet. She makes a notable appearance in only one scene, but Shakespeare makes her memorable by his brilliant exposure of the two sides of the same coin in her personality: brazenness coupled with a capacity for sentimental banter. Her playful teasing of Falstaff is also tempered with a hint of personal concern for him, which lends a gentler dimension to their relationship.

> . . . When wilt thou leave fighting o' days, and foining[1] o' nights, and begin to patch up thine old body for heaven?
>
> (II.iv. 228–30)

---

[1] *foining*: thrusting; usually of a sword, but here with a sexual pun.

46 Ralph Richardson as Falstaff and Joyce Redman as Doll Tearsheet in *Henry IV* Part 2, 1945

Given that this is a middle-aged whore speaking to a fat old man, the words carry a pathos that transcends their surroundings. The same is true of Nell Quickly's farewell to Falstaff:

> ... I have known thee these twenty-nine years, come peascod-time; but an honester, and truer-hearted man,—well, fare thee well.
>
> (II.iv. 379–81)

Here the effect is intensified by the irony that Falstaff is very far from being honest and true-hearted! Her words do not transform his character for us but they do show that in her own way Mistress Quickly, like Doll, loves him, for she is blind to his faults and staunchly loyal to him.

It is a strange experience to turn to *The Merry Wives of Windsor* and find the names of Falstaff and Mistress Quickly among the characters. Not only have they both died during the course of *Henry V*, but these new creations bear very little resemblance to their originals in the Histories. It is an old tradition that Queen Elizabeth asked Shakespeare to write a play showing Falstaff in love, and *The Merry Wives of Windsor* was the result. It is a comedy of remarkable tedium and inconsequence, in which none of the characters emerges with any great mark of individuality. Perhaps this is because the 'comedy' arises essentially from situation and not conflicts of personality. The Mistress Quickly of this play is not hostess of a tavern (there is one, but it is the Garter Inn run by a man), but servant to a Doctor Caius. He is one of the three suitors of Anne Page, and Mistress Quickly claims to 'know Anne's mind'. She is in the centre of gossip in the play, but although she has far more to say and, in a structural sense, plays a more important part than her namesake in the Histories, she emerges as a vapid busybody. When we think of 'Mistress Quickly' this is not the woman we see. It is the Nell of *Henry IV* and *Henry V* whose image springs immediately to mind, as inseparable from Falstaff as the Prince, but more abused and more loyal to him than Hal or any of his cronies.

In *Henry V* Pistol speaks of Doll Tearsheet as 'the lazar kite[2] of Cressid's kind', a reference which makes clear that Cressida would be seen by an Elizabethan audience as the archetypal whore. This certainly is how Shakespeare conceived of her, for within two years he was to write *Troilus and Cressida* where the 'heroine' is as hard, calculating and promiscuous

---

[2] *lazar kite*: disease-ridden bird of prey.

143

47 This Mistress Quickly, played by Mrs Winstanley (1850), who appears in *The Merry Wives of Windsor* has little in common with her namesake who runs the Boar's Head Tavern

as the stereotype of any professional prostitute. The relationship between Troilus and Cressida is founded on sensuality and sexual indulgence, and there is little indication that it ever goes beyond these bounds. The difference between the two of them is that Troilus is demonstrably prepared to be sexually faithful whereas Cressida is not. Within a short time of declaring:

> O you gods divine!
> Make Cressid's name the very crown of falsehood
> If ever she leave Troilus!

(IV.ii. 105–7)

she is enjoying a welcome of kisses from the Greek generals. Her coy teasing of Patroclus is clear evidence that she has no sense of inhibition or shame:

> The kiss you take is better than you give;
> Therefore no kiss!
>
> (IV.v. 38–9)

Such flirtatious banter comes as no surprise. From her first appearance in the play, Cressida's libidinous and shrewdly calculating nature is revealed as her dominant trait.

In Act I Pandarus encourages his niece to let Troilus become her lover. After cracking a few lewd jokes with her uncle (and in Shakespeare's plays coarse speech is always a sign of moral laxity in a woman), Cressida agrees, but in her subsequent soliloquy she leaves the audience in no doubt as to her true intentions: she will keep Troilus in suspense for as long as possible because 'Men price the thing ungain'd more than it is'. Her worldliness contrasts with the naïve eagerness of Troilus, who thinks only of possessing her. When they meet, he asks, in response to her avowal of love: 'Why was my Cressid then so hard to win?' (III.ii. 126). By this time Cressida has discerned that honesty—of a kind—will strike home more forcefully than pretence, for she recognises that Troilus has a simple, open nature and will respond best to what he most wants to hear. Therefore she tells him that she was silent for fear of being thought immodest and also cunningly boosts his ego by suggesting she is so enamoured of Troilus as to reveal any thought to him. In the end she invites him to 'stop my mouth' for she is powerless to resist him. Troilus takes it as the pretty compliment and request for a kiss that Cressida no doubt intends. In her immediate denial of this implication with the histrionic admonition to herself— 'O heavens! What have I done?'—the audience can see that it is clearly a case of 'the lady doth protest too much'. Cressida is testing Troilus' infatuation with her, to feed her vanity. He is completely taken in by her simpering false modesty and equally blind to the fact that she is the one in charge of the situation. The next morning, after a night in bed together, Troilus worries tenderly that Cressida will catch cold by getting up with him as he leaves. He tries to make her stay in bed, but Cressida has a coarse explanation for his kindness:

> You men will never tarry.
> O foolish Cressid! I might have still held off,
> And then you would have tarried.
>
> (IV.ii. 16–18)

145

The crude 'You men' suggests once again that she knows a great deal about sexual behaviour from personal experience. She is therefore revealed as a woman far more base than her nearest counterpart, Doll Tearsheet, because Doll makes no attempt to conceal the fact that she is a whore. There are many indications up to Act II, scene iii, that Cressida is two-faced, which means we cannot possibly accept her protestations of love and fidelity to Troilus at face-value. We are prepared in a way that the simple Troilus is not, even though he bristles when Diomedes, who has come to take her to the Greek camp, openly admires the beautiful Cressida.

Recognition of her true nature is given to Ulysses who watches her kissing the Greek generals:

> There's language in her eye, her cheek, her lip,
> Nay, her foot speaks; her wanton spirits look out
> At every joint and motive of her body.
> (IV.v. 55–7)

Her sensuous beauty inflames every man who sees her, an attribute many a prostitute would envy, and fidelity is meaningless to her for she is an opportunist. Once in the Greek camp, it is in her interest to have a Greek as her lover and protector; hence her acquiescence to Diomede's demands. Above all she is ruled by her senses and she finds the handsome 'honey Greek' Diomede more attractive than Troilus. This offers her excuse enough to forget him, and alone in her tent she murmurs:

> Troilus, farewell! One eye yet looks on thee,
> But with my heart the other eye doth see.
> (V.ii. 103–4)

After this speech she does not appear again and we are left to witness the effects of her treachery on Troilus, who attempts to kill Diomede. His bitter condemnation of Cressida sums her up as a model of perfidy:

> O Cressid! O false Cressid! false, false, false!
> Let all untruths stand by thy stained name,
> And they'll seem glorious.
> (V.ii. 174–6)

In *Henry VI* there is another woman whom Shakespeare clearly intends we should see as a whore, and her identity comes as a shock to the

48 Edith Evans gave a languorous and sensual portrayal of Cressida in 1913

twentieth-century reader more familiar with Shaw's sympathetic portrayal of her. 'Foul fiend of France', 'shameless courtesan' and 'high-minded strumpet', are phrases uttered by the English to describe Joan la Pucelle, Joan of Arc. Such a characterisation would have passed uncensured by an Elizabethan audience and indeed they would have applauded it. The French were old enemies, and the names of their military leaders could be guaranteed to raise a howl of hatred from the groundlings. It was the same in the nineteenth century when, after the French Revolution, Napoleon Bonaparte was known in many English households as the 'bogeyman' of Europe.

Joan is the first of three evil Frenchwomen who threaten the might of England in *Henry VI*, Part 1, the others being the Countess of Auvergne (who tries to trick and trap the English hero Talbot) and Margaret of Anjou (of whom more will be said later). Joan is also symbolic of the treachery and cowardice of the French, and as such is given paper-thin characterisation. There was no need to do otherwise. As a legendary figure she needed no introduction, and a few judicious hints as to the satanic source of her visions and her own immoral nature were sufficient to sway an already prejudiced audience against her.

Two aspects of her initial meeting with the Dauphin immediately suggest that she is not the agent of God's will that the French take her to be. Charles and the Duke of Anjou change places, but Joan knows immediately which is the true Dauphin for '. . . there's nothing hid from me' is her sinister claim to supernatural power. It would be clear to an Elizabethan audience that such arrogance could spring only from contact with evil, rather than good spirits. Secondly, when Charles challenges her to a duel she gladly accepts and within seconds he is crying for mercy. Bearing in mind the Elizabethan—and, of course, Shakespeare's—concept of the hierarchy of nature, the defeat of a man—particularly a man who is a king—by a woman, is fundamentally unnatural. Joan's strength and skill in sword-fighting show that she represents anarchy and that those who follow her cannot prosper.

Proof of both facets is not long in coming. Joan ultimately leads the French to disaster. She conjures up fiends to help her, but they cannot prevail against the righteous power of the English, and Joan is captured. In prison she denies her father and refuses to accept his blessing. His outburst 'O! burn her, burn her! hanging is too good' (V.iv. 33), is a harsh reminder that Joan has committed another crime, perhaps the worst of all: the crime of blatantly refusing to acknowledge and respect her own father. When she realises that her execution by burning is

49 Note the elaborately 'armoured' dress of this eighteenth-century Joan of Arc, played by Mrs Baddeley in 1776

imminent, Joan attempts to save her life by more lies. She claims she is pregnant by the Dauphin, but receiving neither pity nor reprieve, says it was another man and then names yet a third. The English remain unmoved and Joan is taken off to the stake, leaving in a suitably undignified manner and cursing England with her last breath. The

149

implication that she has been prostituting herself with several French noblemen bears out the suggestions earlier in the play made not only by her father (who calls her a 'drab'[3]) but also Talbot. In Act I he neatly sums up the appearance and reality of Joan in a pun on her name:

> Pucelle or puzzel . . .
> Your hearts I'll stamp out with my horse's heels
> (I.iv. 107–8)

he roars out to all Frenchmen, goading his fury with the term they most favour for their leader. 'Pucelle' means 'virgin', but 'puzzel' is Elizabethan English for 'whore', and so her very name betrays her true identity to her enemies.

It is significant that immediately after Joan, that 'foul accursed minister of hell' as the Duke of York calls her, is captured and dragged off, a new danger from France appears in the person of Margaret of Anjou. She enters into a sordid scheme masterminded by the Earl of Suffolk, whereby he arranges her marriage to Henry VI and she becomes his mistress. The burning of Joan is therefore not the end of the French threat. Unwittingly the English have brought a far worse terror upon themselves for Margaret is to become an arch-meddler in internal politics, ultimately helping to precipitate that national catastrophe, the Wars of the Roses.

Margaret is the only character to appear in all three parts of *Henry VI* and in *Richard III*, and she thereby forms a crucial link between the four plays. We witness her appalling change from 'the fairest queen that ever king receiv'd', who charmed Henry VI, to the insane 'wither'd hag', who howls down curses on everyone in Edward IV's court. The ageing-process helps to establish continuity between these plays and also makes us take Margaret more seriously as a character. In her ruthless ambition and the taste for violence and vengeance that eventually lead to madness, she is a prototype of that other terrifying female figure, Lady Macbeth. Unlike this Scottish harridan, however, Margaret had symbolic and social significance because she was a key figure in that period of English history which (for an Elizabethan audience) culminated in the accession of Henry VII, the first Tudor, to the throne. Her fascination lies in the constant reminders of this symbolic

[3] *drab*: whore.

150

significance, coupled with glimpses into the development of her character.

Margaret is the most relentlessly sustained symbol in Shakespeare of all that is unnatural. Only havoc can ensue when the natural order in society (i.e., a monarchy with a strong king in command) is usurped by a weak king allowing a vicious woman to influence his judgement. Shakespeare was sailing very close to the wind with this portrait, because Elizabeth I was monarch when these plays were written. She had been called 'unnatural' for refusing to marry and bear children, and it is perhaps to counter any whispers that the steely Margaret was a caricature that Shakespeare gives the Duke of York a lengthy speech to reveal the precise nature of Margaret's vileness. By the end it is clear that there are no points of comparison between her and Elizabeth I. It is worth looking at this speech in some detail. York has just been captured by Margaret's forces, and she has humiliated him by mocking him and putting a paper crown on his head. She taunts him and, an ultimate cruelty, offers him a napkin dipped in his son's blood so that he may mourn and dry his tears. For her further amusement Margaret tells him to plead his case. His answer is the brilliantly scathing attack which so clearly delineates her symbolic value:

> She-wolf of France, but worse than wolves of France,
> Whose tongue more poisons than the adder's tooth!
> How ill-beseeming is it in thy sex
> To triumph, like an Amazonian trull,
> Upon their woes whom fortune captivates!
> I would assay, proud queen, to make thee blush:
> To tell thee whence thou cam'st, of whom deriv'd,
> Were shame enough to shame thee, wert thou not shameless . . .
> 'Tis beauty that doth oft make women proud;
> But, God he knows thy share thereof is small:
> 'Tis virtue that doth make them most admir'd;
> The contrary doth make thee wonder'd at:
> 'Tis government that makes them seem divine;
> The want thereof makes thee abominable . . .
> O tiger's heart wrapp'd in a woman's hide!
> How couldst thou drain the life-blood of the child,
> To bid the father wipe his eyes withal,
> And yet be seen to bear a woman's face?
> Women are soft, mild, pitiful, and flexible;
> Thou stern, obdurate, flinty, rough, remorseless.
>
> (*3 Henry VI*, I.iv. 111–42)

151

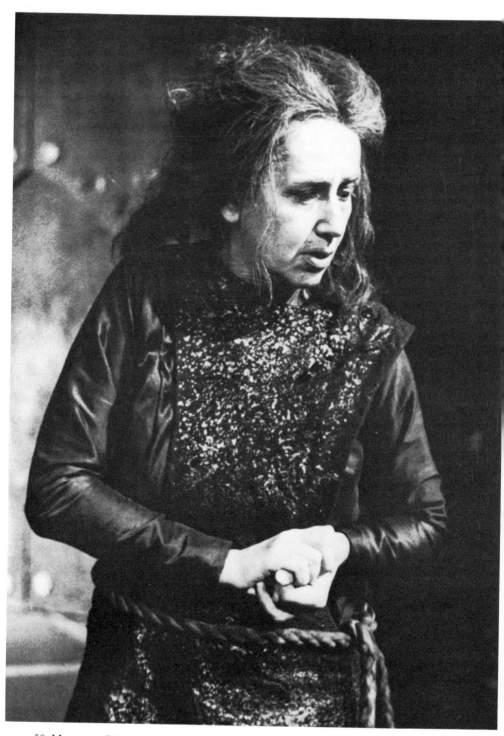

50 Margaret of Anjou appears in all three parts of *Henry VI* and *Richard III*. Ultimately she becomes an insane 'wither'd hag', portrayed here by Dame Peggy Ashcroft in 1963

The last two lines offer the key to the rest. Margaret is totally evil and unnatural because she lacks womanly qualities. In their place she has those that are the glory of a man but grotesque in a woman. (Such at least was the case as it would have appeared to the Elizabethans.) Shakespeare states, through York, that a woman in power is 'admir'd' and even 'divine' if she rules with justice and virtue; a compliment by implication to Elizabeth I. Margaret, by contrast, is 'abominable' because she lacks these qualities. Like Joan of Arc she represents an alien, predatory power, made worse by being female: the 'she-wolf of France'. Like Joan too, she is a 'trull' and 'shameless'; both words ambiguous in Elizabethan English, and both capable of referring to a whore. In Margaret's case it is evident that this is the meaning we are intended to take, for her relationship with Suffolk had, from the first, overtones of adultery. Under the influence of such a creature of evil, both her allies and her enemies are doomed to failure or death. Until we encounter Richmond, the future Henry VII (who emerges after Margaret has left the play), there is no force of sufficient virtue, integrity and true manliness to counteract her dark power and unnaturalness.

As far as the development of Margaret's personality is concerned, from the moment she appears at the end of *Henry VI*, Part 1 there is evidence of her cunning and determination to seize the main chance. She is delighted that Suffolk will arrange her marriage to Henry VI and makes it obvious what his reward will be. She sends Henry:

> a pure unspotted heart,
> Never yet taint with love
> (V.iii. 182–3)

but when Suffolk kisses her and asks if the kiss should be sent too, she replies archly:

> That for thyself: I will not so presume,
> To send such peevish[4] tokens to a king.
> (V.iii. 185–6)

As soon as she arrives in England (*Henry VI*, Part 2) Margaret becomes the focal point of disagreements in court. The terms negotiated by Suffolk for the marriage are disgraceful: Margaret comes with no dowry and England is to give up the very lands in France for which English sol-

---

[4] *peevish*: foolish. To dismiss the kiss so lightly suggests that Margaret is being deliberately insincere, knowing that Suffolk will understand her motives.

diers have died fighting to keep for the king. Henry is deaf to criticism because he is ravished by her beauty. Accordingly the court is split into the king's party (Lancastrians) and opponents of the marriage, headed by the Duke of York (Yorkists). By the end of Act I Margaret is revealed as cruel, ruthless and able to sway the weak Henry in whatever direction she wishes. She effectively takes command, censuring her husband and being publicly disloyal to him:

> Henry my lord is cold in great affairs,
> Too full of foolish pity.
>> (III.i. 224–5)

The growing hatred between the houses of York and Lancaster dominates the latter half of the play, until they meet in open conflict at the battle of St Alban's. York is victorious and in *Henry VI*, Part 3 forces the king to confirm the succession to him. There is a moment approaching comedy, rare in this bleak play, when, having agreed to York's demands, Henry sees Margaret bearing down on him in fury. He is so frightened that he tries to run away from her but she thunders at him: 'Nay, go not from me; I will follow thee!' Henry's attempts to placate her with 'gentle queen' and 'gentle Margaret' only fuel her fire. She rides over his power as a king (by making immediate plans to raise and lead an army) and challenges his rights as a husband (by refusing to eat or sleep with him until the battle is won). Henry does not attempt to assert himself and from now until he is murdered by Richard of Gloucester, Margaret is the effective monarch of England. Her 'reign' is marked by violence and civil disorder; a period of anarchy and senseless killing epitomised by the actions and attitudes of Margaret herself. When eventually York is captured, Margaret first humiliates him (in the scene with the paper crown mentioned earlier) and then stabs him. At the end of this gruesome scene her complete lack of humanity is shown in the grim and sickening joke she makes, as a final mockery of her dead enemy:

> Off with his head, and set it on York gates;
> So York may overlook the town of York.
>> (I.iv. 179–80)

Margaret has such talent as a warrior in battle that she and one of the king's advisers beg Henry to stay away when she is leading the troops, as his presence undermines her leadership! Another reminder that she is 'king' comes where she exhorts the troops before the battle of Tewkes-

bury. Her words are so full of fire and courage that we cannot help but
agree with her son:

> Methinks a woman of this valiant spirit
> Should, if a coward heard her speak these words,
> Infuse his breast with magnanimity,
> And make him, naked, foil a man at arms.
>
> (V.iv. 39–42)

Her triumph is short-lived. The boy who so praised her is killed, Margaret is captured and the battle is lost. The irony of the situation is surely
intentional: nothing Margaret fosters or hopes for can ever come to
good.

In *Richard III* the wars are over, Edward IV is on the throne and Margaret is no longer the warrior 'monarch'. She is old and ugly, a 'foul
wrinkled witch' Richard calls her. There is a demonaic quality in her
now, evident from the outset when she advances menacingly into
Edward's court and denounces his queen, Elizabeth. The bitter hail of
curses which she then showers down on the house of York is Shakespeare's masterpiece of vituperation. It includes a catalogue of insults
directed at Richard, brilliant for its shock-value:

51 Margaret hails down curses on the House of York and on Richard, the future king,
that 'poisonous bunch-back'd toad'. Dame Peggy Ashcroft as Queen Margaret with
Tom Fleming as Buckingham and Ian Holm as Richard III, 1963

Thou elvish-mark'd, abortive, rooting hog!
Thou that wast seal'd in thy nativity
The slave of nature and the son of hell!
Thou slander of thy mother's heavy womb!
Thou loathed issue of thy father's loins!
Thou rag of honour, thou detested . . .
(I.iii. 228–33)

The pounding rhythm is broken only because Margaret is momentarily interrupted but she does not leave her theme and terms Richard 'bottled spider' and 'poisonous bunch-back'd toad', insults that cut home by ridiculing his physical deformity. When at last she goes out, two members of the court confess that their hair stood on end to hear her and their shudder touches us too. Lord Dorset had advised the court, 'Dispute not with her, she is lunatic,' but the explanation is, though partly true, too simple. Margaret's words ring out with the terrible power and conviction of one possessed.

As the play continues, although Margaret does not reappear until near the end of Act IV, her malign presence is constantly sensed as one

52 Elizabeth, wife of Edward IV, 'a beauty-waning and distress'd widow', played here by Brenda Bruce. Norman Rodway plays Richard III, 1970

by one her curses take effect. She herself sums up this hovering in the
wings:

Here in these confines slily have I lurk'd
To watch the waning of mine enemies.
(IV.iv. 3–4)

In the ensuing scene Margaret is joined by Queen Elizabeth, whose
husband and sons (the 'Princes in the Tower') have been murdered by
Richard, and the Duchess of York whose husband was stabbed to death
by Margaret. The three make a bizarre trio, aged crones lamenting their
dead in elaborate litany:

Q. Mar.   I had an Edward, till a Richard kill'd him;
          I had a Harry, till a Richard kill'd him;
          Thou hadst an Edward till a Richard kill'd him;
          Thou hadst a Richard till a Richard kill'd him.
Duch.   I had a Richard too, and thou didst kill him,
          I had a Rutland too, thou holp'st to kill him.
(IV.iv. 40–5)

The very formal pattern of the language has been cited by some critics as
an example of Shakespeare at his worst: stiff, stilted and almost incomprehensible. Surely the truth is otherwise. The point of this scene is that
the mourning of these three old women represents not only the end of
hostility between the houses of York and Lancaster, but that the horrors
endured are beyond description. The only language appropriate to the
moment is plain, dignified and ritualised. The tone is sustained until
Richard's entrance, by which time Margaret has made her final exit. We
never hear of her death, a fact that reinforces our impression in the
earlier part of the play that she is still present, looking on. It is surely no
accident that when Margaret prays Richard may die she adds: 'That I
may live to say "The dog is dead".' There is an eerie echo in Richmond's
words of triumph at the end of the play: 'The day is ours, the bloody dog
is dead.'

As Margaret is the supreme example of what far-reaching evils can
result when a ruthless woman is in power, so Volumnia exemplifies the
undermining influence one woman can have on one man. In her case it is
not as wife or queen, but as mother.

157

53 Sheila Burrell successfully captured the demonaic power of Margaret in this production of *Richard III* in 1970

She is not the only 'mother' figure in the Histories and allied plays. In a number of them relationships are sketched between mothers and sons, sometimes with considerable pathos, as with Constance, mother of Arthur in *King John*. Volumnia, however, is not merely a mother but a Roman matriarch. Her son, the General Coriolanus, is so governed by her that he allows her pleas to affect an important political decision—one that ultimately costs him his life.

Volumnia is contrasted with the gentle Virgilia, Coriolanus' wife. She constantly fears for her husband, whereas his mother is only concerned that he should fight honourably. If she had a dozen sons, she claims:

> ... I had rather had eleven die nobly for their country than one voluptuously surfeit out of action.
>
> (I.iii. 24–5)

Virgilia is sickened and appalled at the thought of Coriolanus being wounded, but Volumnia glories in the gashes he has received in battle:

> I' the shoulder, and i' the left arm: there will be large cicatrices[5] to show the people when he shall stand for his place. He received in the repulse of Tarquin seven hurts i' the body.
>
> (II.i. 144–7)

At times her awed tone betrays that she sees him as a Colossus, a god:

> Death, that dark spirit, in's nervy arm doth lie;
> Which being advanc'd, declines, and then men die!
> (II.i. 157–8)

It is no surprise that when Coriolanus returns triumphant to Rome it is his mother who is the first to greet him. Virgilia weeps in her happiness, but Coriolanus chides her—it is his mother's impassioned, adoring welcome that he wants.

Volumnia and Coriolanus' friends are eager for their hero to become Consul as the crowning glory to his achievements. Unfortunately Coriolanus upsets the citizens of Rome by his abrupt way of asking for their vote and then by losing his temper with them. They are enraged and demand his death. Coriolanus (rescued by his friends) is equally incensed and refuses to return, cap in hand, to them. All seems lost, but Volumnia persuades him to apologise to the mob, telling him the very words he can use to mollify them without sacrificing his integrity. Her

---

[5] *cicatrices*: scars.

54 One of the few memorable characters in *King John* is Constance, devoted mother of Prince Arthur, played here by Mrs Barry, 1775

method is to appeal to his patriotism and his loyalty to her, implying that he will let both country and family down if he does not become a Consul. On this basis, she argues, it is not hypocritical to use mild words to win over the plebeians:

> this no more dishonours you at all
> Than to take in a town with gentle words . . .
> I would dissemble with my nature where
> My fortunes and my friends at stake requir'd
> I should do so in honour.
>
> (III.ii. 58–9 and 62–4)

Her argument is irresistible. Against his better judgement, Coriolanus gives in but within moments of appearing before the people in the Forum he loses his temper with the malicious tribunes and bellows at everyone there:

> You common cry of curs' whose breath I hate
> As reek o' the rotten fens.
>
> (III.iii. 120–1)

He is banished and joins forces with an old enemy, Aufidius, to attack Rome. In his fury for revenge on the city that has spurned him he is deaf to the pleas of his old friends. It is only when his mother begs him to call off the attack and kneels on 'no softer cushion than the flint', that he relents. In a long speech she uses the same method as when she persuaded him to return to the Forum: a heady appeal to honour and patriotism, laced with emotional blackmail. At the end she pretends to admit defeat but leaves him with the appalling vision of burning his wife, child and mother to death. Coriolanus is at first too distraught to speak and can only hold Volumnia by the hand. At last he bursts out:

> O my mother! mother! O!
> You have won a happy victory to Rome;
> But for your son, believe it, O! believe it,
> Most dangerously you have with him prevailed,
> If not most mortal to him.
>
> (V.iii. 182–6)

He has capitulated, but his words are prophetic. Having withdrawn his troops he goes with Aufidius, who calls him traitor and has him killed by conspirators. Although part of the reason for Coriolanus' ignominious end must be his own nature, because he is so hot-headed and tactless, the circumstances that lead to his death have been engineered by his mother. It is she who persuades him to go to the Forum in the first place, she who insists he apologise to the people and she who makes him go back on his word to Aufidius. The play is fraught with irony, for Coriolanus, the Roman hero adored by his mother, dies dishonourably, out of Rome, and as a direct result of Volumnia's influence. Although the penitent Aufidius swears that 'he shall have a noble memory', we cannot help feeling that Coriolanus' death was lamentably unjust. The worst of it is that Volumnia always advised her son from the highest possible motives and an undoubted, almost suffocating, affection. It is the tragedy of a particular kind of blindness unique in Shakespeare.

55 Coriolanus is completely dominated by his mother, Volumnia, played here by Dame Sybil Thorndike, 1938. Ironically it is her concern for his welfare that leads to his tragic death

Virgilia, Coriolanus' wife, played very much second fiddle to his mother. It seems to be the case in the History and other plays within this group that unless a wife has some other facet of influence and power (such as Queen Margaret) her role does not interest Shakespeare sufficiently for him to suggest significance for it in its own right. For these women— invariably minor characters—he follows the stereotype of his age. The good wives (and there is a long list of them) are patient, faithful and loving, like Calpurnia and Portia in *Julius Caesar*, or Lady Percy in *Henry IV*, Part 1. The few bad wives are fickle and bold-faced, like Helen in *Troilus and Cressida*. Even in *The Merry Wives of Windsor*, which focuses on a dreary intrigue among a group of married women, the two chief gossips, Mistress Ford and Mistress Page, conform to the basic pattern of the 'good wife'.

This adherence to a pattern, seen most clearly with the wives but also evident in the other female archetypes mentioned in this chapter, gives the women of the Histories and related plays a particular importance. Although literary and dramatic significance for many of them is negligible, their creation springs from the mind of a man imbued with the social attitudes and prejudices of his age. They therefore form an extra-ordinary and invaluable guide to Elizabethan ideas. Those who, like Queen Margaret and Volumnia, have personalities that do crack the shell of their stereotypes, leap out at us as fully-fledged characters, and even vie with the men for our attention.

V

Shakespeare's Women on Stage

> Suit the action to the word, the word
> to the action.
>
> *Hamlet* III.ii. 19–20

Given the tremendous range and variety of female roles that Shakespeare created, it is strange to realise that he would never have witnessed even one played by a real woman. The delicate Juliet, sluttish Doll Tearsheet, matronly Volumnia—all these, together with the host of other women in the plays, were designed for, and acted by, boys. At the time Shakespeare was writing actresses were known on the continental stage, but it was a fashion frowned on by the English, who stuck conservatively to the tradition of male actors only. Apart from one or two daring appearances, which were very much the exception to a stern rule, no woman was to tread the boards of an English theatre until the 1660s.

In Shakespeare's day acting companies were relatively new entities and the profession was regarded with much suspicion. Until the 1570s, when the first theatres were built, actors were simply travelling players. With few responsibilities and always on the move, their reputation for drinking, fighting and whoring was far greater than that for their art. They proved such a headache for the authorities that in 1572 an 'Acte for the punishment of Vacabondes' was passed, largely to control the players, who were classed with other wanderers and entertainers, like pedlars, tinkers and bear-baiters. The Act pinned them down, because from this time on players had to have an official authorisation from a member of the nobility to be allowed to act. In consequence, public theatres sprang up in London to house the rival groups and the profession became legitimate. It was still not completely respectable, however, in spite of active support from the chief arbiter of morality and good taste, Queen Elizabeth. Fairly or not, actors inherited the stigma of loose-living from their predecessors. One aspect of their ill-fame is of particular interest since it concerns women. Prostitutes were always hovering around wherever the groups of itinerant players settled for a few nights, and some would even travel along with the troupe. The association of such women with acting probably provides an additional reason why a life on the stage was regarded as highly improper for any Elizabethan lady.

By modern standards, an Elizabethan theatre company was small. For most of his career Shakespeare belonged to the Chamberlain's Men, which numbered about eight men and two or three boys. It is not clear how recruitment was organised but possibly the theatre managers established links with schools which could then give likely boys a prod in the direction of the stage. Some of the richer schools, such as Eton, even had their own companies made up entirely of boys. There was a vogue throughout the Elizabethan era for seeing children on stage and eleven of the thirty-five theatre companies in existence by 1590 had no adult members apart from the manager. In such companies the boys acted in male and female roles and the audience delighted in seeing such precocious children performing in 'adult' plays, which thereby became curiosities in their own right, reduced to a miniature scale. Stage prodigies—or little monsters, as they must have seemed to the adult actors who had to compete with them—held more than a passing

56 The Bateman sisters, Ellen and Kate, were child-actors who drew large audiences in the mid-nineteenth century. They are seen here as Richard III and Richmond, 1851

fascination. Although the boys' companies were disbanded in the seventeenth century, child-actors continue to emerge from time to time and draw large audiences. In our own century the focus on juvenile stage-presence has shifted from the theatre to the cinema and popular music, but the nature of the attraction is the same. Shirley Temple is possibly the outstanding example, but more recent years have spawned whole groups of child-performers, sometimes all from one family, such as the singing group The Osmonds. The film *Bugsy Malone* used an entire cast of children and was a huge box-office success. Their hold over audiences, like that of the Elizabethan boys' companies is not just because they represent a departure from the norm, but rather because their fame, by its very nature, must be short-lived. Old age sharpens its scythe quietly but strikes the child prodigy at about fifteen. He may be totally lost to the public memory by the time he is twenty.

None of the companies Shakespeare worked for exploited this taste for the ephemeral viewed from the wrong end of the telescope. The boy-actors were what was accepted and expected for the parts they played. Once their beards sprouted and their voices dropped, they could then move on to male roles. For the talented actor, there was thus a career-structure in the Elizabethan and Jacobean theatre that could last from his tenth year until his death. With luck, he might even end up holding shares in the company.

When a boy came to a company he was immediately apprenticed to an established actor who was then responsible for training him. The process was long and taxing, for the boy would have to learn not only to speak effectively and make his presence felt on stage, but also to dance, sing and play various musical instruments. The emphasis seems to have been on his versatility and the need to work well with the other members of the company, for as yet there was no 'star' billing for individual talents.

This is hardly surprising, for the accusations of lascivious tastes and riotous behaviour which were levelled at the actors helped to unite them into a closely-knit community. Internal squabbling and back-biting about who was who within the company-hierarchy would have made their lives impossibly fraught. Such calculated and invidious narcissism is possible only when the presence of an adoring audience assures the actors of a secure public image. This could not be the case with the Elizabethan and Jacobean companies, and we do not even know the names of most of the actors.

In Shakespeare's company there may well have been boys who were

166

57 Thomas Betterton as Hamlet with possibly Mary Saunderson as Gertrude, 1709, in the closet-scene from Rowe's edition of Shakespeare

better suited to one type of role than another and for whom Shakespeare tailored particular parts. Beatrice, Rosalind and Viola, for example, were created within a three-year period and have sufficient similarity to suggest that Shakespeare had a special boy in mind to play them. Intriguing though such thoughts are, they must unfortunately remain speculative, for there is no evidence of Shakespeare's intentions beyond what is in the plays themselves and they do not give away any secrets about individual actors.

We can turn to the plays for information of a more general nature, and that is, whether Shakespeare shaped his female roles in any particular way, knowing that they were to be played by boys rather than women. We then find that here, as in so many other areas, he transcends what might well have proved a restrictive convention. There is virtually nothing to indicate the playwright's awareness that he was writing women's parts for youthful female-impersonators, beyond an avoidance of any physical display of passion or eroticism on stage. Other reasons can be found for this, but it just might have been Shakespeare's conscious policy not to burden a boy with the requirement to perform actions that would seem beyond the range of his own experience and might reduce the role to a parody. In terms of impact on an audience Shakespeare must have had the effect of his boys' true identity in mind when he wrote many of the Comedies, for six of his heroines change into doublet and hose. There is a special comic conundrum in this situation because the boy-actor is now the closest he can get to being his real self on stage, yet it has come about through two layers of disguises: the boy impersonates the woman who is impersonating a boy.

It is difficult to imagine just how the boys played their roles since we have little information about acting styles until well into the seventeenth century. Since their success depended on sharing an illusion of their femaleness with the audience, the chances are that they did not aim for a true-to-life representation of a woman's voice and mannerisms for fear of being laughed at. A guffaw in the wrong place can destroy dramatic tension and ruin the best moments of a play, and so the boys were probably trained to adopt rather stylised feminine gestures which would seem artificial to us.

The English would no doubt have given in sooner or later to the fashion of having women on stage. In *The Ball*, a play performed in London in 1639, a character speaks of the French stage:

Yet the women are the best actors, they play
Their own parts, a thing much desir'd in England.

168

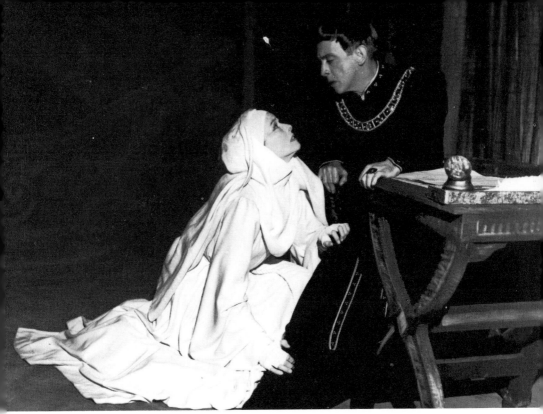

58 Shakespeare's plays have delighted audiences for over two hundred years in America, which has produced an impressive number of Shakespearian actresses. One of the best known is Katharine Hepburn, here playing Isabella to Robert Helpmann's Angelo. America's early encouragement of touring companies had a profound effect on both sides of the Atlantic. This production of *Measure for Measure* was in that tradition, being one of three plays performed on the Old Vic Australian Tour, 1955

Presumably he was voicing an opinion which many shared, though when a French company *did* play in London in 1629, using women on stage, the audience reacted violently. As soon as the actresses appeared there was uproar. Whistling, hooting and stamping, the affronted audience even threw rotten fruit at the women until 'pippin-pelted', as a contemporary records, they were driven off. Probably there were many arguments about the comparative merits of boys and actresses, but within a few years the audiences had no choice at all, for in 1642 Parliament ordered the closure of all theatres.

The Puritans saw the theatres as dens of 'theft and whoredom, pride and prodigality, villainy and blasphemy', and once Cromwell was in power little time was lost before drama was forbidden. Entertainment was permitted, but only of a kind that the Puritans felt could not disturb the morals or passions of the audience. Shakespeare's plays were out, the puppet-shows and innocent diversions like bear-baiting were in. If the meaning of a play was sufficiently diluted and disguised by music, it was

169

59 Katharine Hepburn, here playing Rosalind to William Prince's Orlando, exemplifies the tie that frequently exists in America between the theatre and Shakespeare studies at university. She attended Bryn Mawr College before becoming a professional actress

permissible, and some strange deformities of Shakespeare's plays emerged, adapted in this way to keep within the law.

In 1642 some eight theatres prospered in London. The Act of Closure meant that a large group of actors was unemployed, had no base and was unable to continue with the training of boys for women's parts. The actors were indignant and the following year produced a pamphlet entitled 'The Actors Remonstrance, or, Complaint . . . for the Silencing of their Profession, and Banishment of their severall Playhouses'. The authors pleaded particularly on behalf of the boys who '. . . . ere we shall have libertie to act againe, will be grown out of use like cract organ pipes, and have faces as old as our flags'. But Parliament was unmoved. The actors were soon scattered, some enlisting and others fleeing to the Continent.

The year 1660 saw the restoration not only of a monarch, but also of the theatre. After eighteen years, 'straight' drama was allowed once more, although it was restricted by royal patent to two companies. These were the King's Company at the Theatre Royal, Drury Lane, under the management of Thomas Killigrew, and the Duke of York's Company at Dorset Garden Theatre, with Sir William Davenaunt as manager. Exiled actors flocked home, but there were now, as they had predicted in 1643, no boys trained for the women's parts. Boys who had been trained by 1642 were now at least thirty years old and their attempts at impersonating women must have been very funny. Thomas Jordan wrote a Prologue to a production of *Othello* in 1660 where he laughingly censures these lumbering 'boys':

> Our women are defective and so sized
> You'd think they were some of the guard, disguis'd,
> For, to speak truth, men act, that are between
> Forty and fifty, wenches of fifteen.
> With bone so large, and nerve so incompliant,
> When you call DESDEMONA, enter GIANT!'

Embarrassing incidents could also occur. A play which Charles II was watching at Drury Lane suddenly and inexplicably stopped in the middle of a scene. After waiting impatiently in his box for some minutes the King sent a message to find out the cause of the delay. A harassed theatre manager replied that the heroine was not yet ready to come on stage because he was still shaving!

The solution to the problem was to have women play the women's parts. Actors and managers who had been abroad had seen the French and Italian actresses and therefore many who returned were favourably disposed to the idea. Charles' court, so fashion-conscious and eager to dispel the Puritan gloom of the past eighteen years, would not want to be thought out of date and so the stage was truly set for the appearance of the first professional actress.

The occasion of her début was 8 December 1660 in the production of *Othello* at Drury Lane. She played Desdemona, as testified in Jordan's Prologue:

> I come, unknown to any of the rest,
> To tell you news; I saw the lady drest:
> The woman plays today; mistake me not,
> No man in gown, nor page in petticoat:
> A woman to my knowledge.

But who was she? There is no cast-list for this production and various

60 Peg Woffington, great comic actress and mistress of David Garrick, as Mistress Ford, 1743

names have been suggested over the years. The most likely claimant is Margaret Hughes. Her name appears in a cast-list for *Othello* in 1669, and in spite of the nine-year interval this may well indicate that she was the first female Desdemona. At that time there was a custom of 'giving' a part to the first actor or actress who played it successfully. No one else in the company would be allowed to play it unless its 'owner' was ill, retired or dead. Within just a few months of the first English woman, whoever she was, stepping onto the professional stage, actresses were taking part in plays at both of the theatres. A royal patent issued to the managers, Killigrew and Davenaunt, in 1662 reflects their rapid progress:

> We do likewise permit and give leave that all the women's parts to be acted in either of the said two companies ... may be performed by women, so long as these recreations ... may ... be esteemed not only harmless delights, but useful and instructive representations of human life ...

It is ironic, given the lofty wording of this document, that these early actresses gained considerable notoriety for their off-stage activities. Acting was the newest profession for a woman, but many of them were also engaged in the oldest. Margaret Hughes, for example, openly flaunted her position as Prince Rupert's mistress. Unlike the situation in Elizabethan and Jacobean times, the Restoration theatres had little support from the public and provided entertainment essentially for the court. This meant that the attractive women who now flocked onto the stage were easy prey for wealthy aristocrats in search of a more glamorous alliance than could be found in the back-street brothels. For a small fee, men were allowed to go behind scenes or hang about in the wings while the play was on in the hope of being the first to accost an actress as she came off-stage. Such blatant propositioning may seem incredible to us, but dissolute living was increasingly a feature of the age, and the cheerful amorality of many of the actresses reflects it.

Whatever may have gone on in their private lives, once on stage the actresses were capable of superlative performances. Of the two companies allowed to produce plays it was primarily Davenaunt's that specialised in Shakespeare and possessed the leading Shakespearian actress of the day. Her name was Mary Saunderson (later known as Mary Betterton for she married the male lead in the company, Thomas Betterton).

For twenty years Mary Saunderson trod the boards in the Duke of York's Company and played an impressive number of Shakespearian roles. She was only just beaten for the title of first English actress by the

173

woman who played Desdemona in 1660. Early in 1661 she became the first woman Ophelia and a little later the first Juliet. For her contemporaries, her most impressive role was Lady Macbeth. Colley Cibber, theatre manager, writer and critic, wrote after her death of how she could 'throw out those quick and careless Strokes of Terror from the Disorder of a guilty mind' in her interpretation of the part. She was remarkable in another way too, for Cibber adds: 'She was a Woman of an unblemish'd and sober life, a faithful companion to her husband.' There is no other Shakespearian actress of her calibre until the following century. The King's Company boasted Anne Marshall and Margaret Hughes, both famous in their day, but they were more frequently seen in plays by Jonson, Fletcher, or the host of new Restoration playwrights. Nell Gwynn also belonged to this company, but although her saucy charm and pretty face made many an aristocratic heart beat faster, she cannot be considered as a serious actress.

From what we can gather from contemporary accounts, late seventeenth-century actresses and actors went in for what may be termed 'personality' acting. That is to say they tended to impose an image of themselves on the audience's mind and memory, rather than that of the characters they impersonated. In keeping with this self-conscious projection the costumes of the women were incredibly opulent and bizarre. There was no attempt at historical accuracy in their choice of dress; they wore 'modern' dress, tricked out with huge plumes, ruffles and jewellery, often topped by an enormous coloured wig. Such extravagance was far more exciting than the clothes most of them could afford for themselves and so, understandably, they liked to parade in public in their stage-attire. A costume that could stand up to fifty performances of Cleopatra could be ruined by one night at a royal ball, and there were many fierce arguments between the money-conscious theatre managers and the wayward actresses. Matters came to a head in 1675 when an agreement was signed in both companies, forbidding women to wear their costumes outside the theatre premises.

The presence of actresses brought about a revolution in the English theatre that changed its character for ever. It is fortunate that the other revolution on the Restoration stages, the butchering of Shakespeare's text, did not have a similar long-term effect. Even so, it comes as a shock to realise that audiences have only been sure of hearing the words that Shakespeare wrote, uncut and without additions, for barely a century. For well over two hundred years Shakespeare's true text was effectively lost.

61 Sarah Siddons, perhaps the greatest Shakespearian actress in history, as Lady Macbeth in 1812

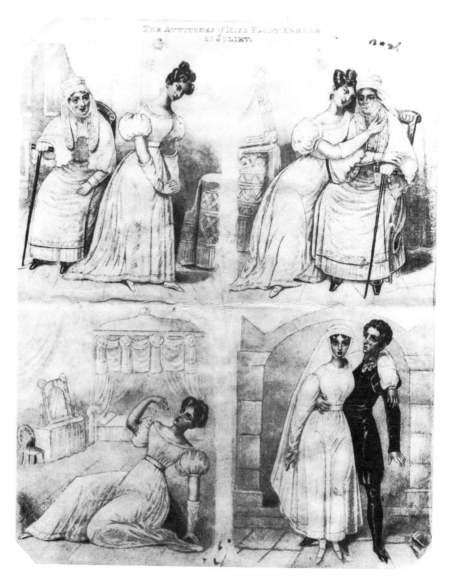

62 Sketches of Fanny Kemble's performance as Juliet at Covent Garden, 1829

To prune, lop and graft onto the works of a genius seems the height of criminal arrogance, but that was not how it appeared to the literary men of the Restoration. Their attitude to Shakespeare was that while much of his poetry and characterisation was unquestionably brilliant, the construction of his plays left a great deal to be desired. His work seemed untidy and inelegant in an age when the vogue was for polished

63 Mrs Bunn, wife of the business-minded manager of Drury Lane and Covent Garden, as Hermione in *The Winter's Tale*, 1823

symmetry rather than realism. Shakespeare's concept of tragedy—that the innocent were frequently destroyed with the guilty—also bothered them. They wanted serious drama to portray a clear social and Christian moral, where the good or penitent were rewarded and the bad punished. Comedy too, should have its roots in social behaviour. It is this kind of expectation which no doubt lay behind Samuel Pepys'

64 Lillie Langtry as Cleopatra in 1890, famous more as Edward VII's mistress than for her ability as an actress

comment on *A Midsummer Night's Dream*, that he found it: 'the most insipid, ridiculous play that ever I saw in my life.'

Restoration attitudes were equally ambivalent to Shakespeare's women characters. From what we can gather about life in Charles' court, women were seen as pretty toys for men's pleasure and were certainly not accorded respect as individuals. Women characters in a serious play were expected to be gentle, sober and pure, exemplifying the age-old stereotype of 'femininity'. Roles such as Lady Macbeth and Queen Margaret, both ruthless women, were considerably watered down to fit in with contemporary tastes. There is no getting away from their evil influence, even so, and it must have come as a relief to the audiences that they both die insane.

Shakespeare was regarded with sufficient reverence for there to be restrictions on who was allowed to meddle with his works. The Duke's Company manager, Davenaunt, was allowed to 'reform' the plays so that they would be suitable for the refined tastes of his audience. He cut out scenes which he felt were offensive or, on the other hand, involved too much metaphorical language. Sometimes he completely changed the nature of a play, even altering its name. In Davenaunt's hands *Measure for Measure* becomes *The Law Against Lovers*. Mariana is missed out altogether and Isabella ends up happily engaged to Angelo, a hero in this version. A sub-plot is added for pleasing symmetry, involving a younger brother of Angelo's. A similar ironing out of pains and doubts occurs in *Much Ado About Nothing*, in which Beatrice and Benedick are shown as a loving couple from the start. One of the most famous poets of the age, John Dryden, also adapted Shakespeare for the stage. *Troilus and Cressida* appears in 1679 as Dryden's *Truth Found Too Late*, with a remarkable change from the original in that Cressida is faithful. His version of *Anthony and Cleopatra* (*All for Love*) reduced the heroine to a sentimental caricature of her true self.

Of all the seventeenth century adaptations of Shakespeare, perhaps the most notorious is Nahum Tate's *The History of King Lear* of 1680. Tate attacked the text with crusading ardour, removing or distorting much of the poetry and altering the tragic course of the play. In his version Lear is restored to his kingdom, and Cordelia marries Edgar. The happy ending appealed to generations of play-goers and the original text was not seen again until 1830. Even as great and sensitive a critic as Dr Johnson supported Tate's version because it showed 'the final triumph of persecuted virtue'. He adds: 'I was many years ago so shocked by Cordelia's death, that I know not whether I ever endured to read again the last scenes of the play till I undertook to revise them as an editor.'

The drastic interference with Shakespeare's plays had a profound effect on the women's roles. They were forced to conform to an externally-imposed standard of what the adapters felt human behaviour *should* be rather than what it is. It is ironic to recall Hamlet's words to the players on the purpose of acting, which can surely be taken to apply to the purpose of drama itself. It 'was and is, to hold, as' twere, the mirror up to nature'. Such was not the concern of Dryden or Tate, and because of the prevailing idealised image of women as gentle, unimportant little things, the female characters come off the worst. The great step forward that had been taken by the introduction of women to the stage was severely countered by the gutless Shakespearian parts they were given to play. It is much to the credit of that irrepressible group of early actresses—Mary Saunderson, Margaret Hughes, Anne Marshall, the 'matchless' Mrs Bracegirdle and a host of others—that they were able to move audiences so much by their interpretation of Shakespeare's heroines as 'refined' by a Dryden or a Tate.

But in one way the actresses were exceptionally fortunate. The more Shakespearian roles they played the more they were considered to be in the bracket of 'serious' artists. From the mid-1660s a fashion sprang up for plays performed by an all-women cast. This was to cater for the salacious tastes of an all-male audience, who liked to see the actresses in tight-fitting jackets and breeches, and stockings that revealed the shapely legs normally hidden in public. The plays they performed were packed with obscene jokes and the actresses who took part in them soon had a reputation for encouraging immorality. Women were also blamed, simply because they were present among the cast, for the low tone of plays that used children. Towards the end of the century this was a new and unpleasant fashion. Small children, usually girls of seven or eight would come on stage before the play started to sing a bawdy song or speak an obscene prologue. Their innocence and ignorance of the meaning much enhanced the pleasure imparted to the audience. Moralists strongly attacked such practices, but were unable or unwilling to censure their fellow men for creating a demand for such plays. They could see, however, that the sudden taste for risqué productions coincided with the coming of women to the stage, and so they pounced on the actresses as scape-goats.

In the eighteenth century the two patent theatres were rebuilt to house larger audiences. After a period when their whole future seemed in jeopardy (they were forced to unite in 1682 in order to keep going at all

65 Millicent Bandmann-Palmer as Hamlet, 1895

66 Bella Pateman as Hamlet, 1880

67 Sarah Bernhardt as Hamlet, 1899

68 Esme Beringer as Romeo, 1896

because the audiences were so small), the managers put on a wider variety of plays in order to attract the public purse. The old adaptations of Shakespeare continued to appear but they were joined by others designed to fill the theatres. The actor-manager Colly Cibber's rewriting of *Richard III* in 1700 was of this kind. He added scenes of gratuitous violence and a strong love-interest to the plot. Elizabeth of York, mentioned only by name in the original, appears in the flesh and much emphasis is placed on the Earl of Richmond's courtship of her.

Until the appearance of Sarah Siddons in the last quarter of the century, there are only two Shakespearian actresses of note after the retirement of Mary Saunderson and her contemporaries. The first of these, in fame if not ability, was Peg Woffington, mistress of that extraordinary actor, manager, director and dramatist David Garrick. Largely because of her amorous friendship with Garrick, Peg Woffington's name became attached to many scandals during her lifetime. In fact she seems to have been genuinely devoted to him and to the theatre, giving material and moral support to young actors, actresses and promising playwrights. Her great strength as an artist lay in comedy, and she played many Shakespearian roles, including Portia, Rosalind, Viola, Helena and Mistress Ford. Also in Garrick's company was the great tragic actress Hannah Pritchard. She kept out of emotional tangles with him, but was much influenced by his style of acting. Garrick aimed for naturalism in his roles, a strong contrast with the 'personality' acting of the previous generation. Hannah Pritchard, using this new technique, played Lady Macbeth to such perfection that those who saw them both, said her interpretation was second only to Sarah Siddons. Garrick had other influences on theatrical tradition which were a boon for the actresses. He was the first manager to have the courage to end the custom of allowing men backstage during the course of a play, which meant that actresses could give professional and complete attention to their roles. He also stopped the audience from sitting on the stage, a practice that had frequently caused disruptions in previous years. If they got carried away they were quite likely to leave their seats and join in the action. Men sometimes strolled right onto the stage to make sure the actresses noticed them! Garrick was also firm about discipline within the company. The old practice had been that parts for a new play were shared out on the basis of whoever pushed hardest and clamoured loudest was given the best. He insisted on selecting those he felt would be right for each part.

There can have been little doubt that Sarah Siddons was the best when she came to Drury Lane. Today she is considered perhaps the greatest Shakespearian actress in history. Her magic lay partly in her extraordinary versatility, for she played comic, historical and tragic heroines with equal conviction, electrifying her audiences. She also offered a new image for the actress, having an air of dignity and composure both on and off stage which impressed those who met her. Her demeanour forced the public to take her profession much more seriously. She was also a lasting influence in terms of theatre-practice, for she insisted on doing away with the frills and fripperies of costume used by her predecessors. Instead she wore elegantly simple clothes which encouraged the audience to pay attention to the character she was playing, undistracted by what she wore. Sometimes audiences were distracted by events which had nothing to do with the actresses. In 1809 Mrs Siddons' brother, John Kemble, tried to raise the price of tickets to the new Covent Garden Theatre of which he was manager. All hell was let loose. Although Mrs Siddons was playing Lady Macbeth, one of her most famous roles, the audience rioted every night for two months. The noise of their shrieks, whistles and brawls was so dreadful that the play could be performed only in mime, for not a word was audible. Finally Kemble gave in and sold tickets at the old prices. We can only be amazed by her courage to have braved so many terrible evenings on stage.

Her career was long and successful, and some years before she died at the age of seventy-six, in 1831, her successor in artistic terms was seen as the Irish Eliza O'Neill. Her name is little known today, but she thrilled nineteenth-century audiences, particularly by her interpretations of the 'purer' and less complex Shakespearian heroines such as Juliet and Isabella. Fanny Kemble, a member of the great theatrical family and niece of Sarah Siddons, was also a notable Juliet. She was one of the first actresses to gain a reputation on both sides of the Atlantic, for she made frequent appearances on the American stage. But not everybody liked her. The theatre manager Charles Macready noted in his diary that he had never met anyone 'so bad, so unnatural, so affected, so conceited'.

Although Eliza O'Neill and Fanny Kemble performed Shakespearian roles, they were among the few actresses to have the opportunity to do so. During this period there was a dearth of theatre managers who were interested in producing Shakespearian plays. The decline in artistic standards and appreciation of traditional drama was reflected in the appointment of one Alfred Bunn. He was for two years joint manager of Drury Lane and Covent Garden (which had replaced

69 Visitors to London in the 1840s could see the Cushman sisters, Charlotte and Susan
as Romeo and Juliet at the Haymarket Theatre

the old Dorset Garden Theatre). His interests were more financial than aesthetic if we can believe the accounts of contemporary play-goers. They tell us that actors and actresses were often employed, no doubt to save money, at both theatres at once. This meant that after the early performance at Drury Lane the streets would suddenly be thronged with players in full costume, rushing breathlessly to get to Covent Garden in time to perform in the other play!

What made a great difference was the ending in 1843 of the royal patent which had given these two theatres a monopoly in 'legitimate' drama for a hundred and eighty-three years. The Haymarket, until then a small, insignificant theatre, was refurbished and emerged as the most glamorous place of entertainment in London. The managers favoured Shakespeare's plays and many famous actresses were to be seen there, including the Cushman sisters, Charlotte and Susan, who were famed for their performances as Romeo and Juliet.

The opening of this theatre together with the influence of theatre managers like Macready, whose production of *King Lear* in 1830 restored the original text, and Edmund Kean, who specialised in Shakespearian roles, mean that Shakespeare's plays were given a new lease of life from about the mid-nineteenth century. There was also an increasing taste for sentimentality on the stage, which meant that the focus tended to shift from the actors to the actresses, even in Shakespearian drama. The desire for simple naturalism fostered by Garrick and Mrs Siddons, gave way to a melodramatic, declamatory style designed to arouse the tender emotions of the audience. Victorian actresses are all marked to a greater or lesser extent by this trait, even the most famous of them all, Ellen Terry.

Friend of Bernard Shaw, wit, writer and outstanding actress, Ellen Terry became leading lady at the Lyceum in 1878. She portrayed most of Shakespeare's heroines including Lady Macbeth, whose character she conveyed as calculating and cruel, masked on the outside by an exotic costume. In an age that had only recently had the chance of hearing Shakespeare's texts unadulterated by the meddlings of other writers, such an interpretation was new and exciting. Ellen Terry was particularly praised for the sleep-walking scene, in which she gave Lady Macbeth's fatal madness pathos and a chilling reality. It was the perfect combination for Victorian sensibilities, inclined to sentiment on the one hand and a fascination with death on the other. In her memoirs she gives her own definition of what qualities an actress should possess: 'Imagination, industry and intelligence—the Three I's—are all

70 Madame Vestris as Oberon, 1840. Her legs became so famous that plaster casts of them were sold as souvenirs

71 A Russian interpretation of Cleopatra: Ludmilla Storozheva at the Grodno Drama Theatre, 1964

indispensable to the actress, but of the three the greatest is, without any doubt, imagination.' Ellen Terry was a brilliant exponent of her own philosophy, delighting audiences in both England and America.

Her contemporary, Lillie Langtry, was also famous, but more for being Edward VII's mistress than for her ability on stage. Audiences flocked to see her largely out of curiosity and to marvel at her delicate beauty. In 1890 she appeared as Cleopatra, but in spite of her physical charms her performance was so excrutiatingly inept that a review ridiculing her appeared in *Punch*. Dissatisfied members of the audience would have had little trouble in finding a better Shakespearian actress elsewhere. In the last quarter of the nineteenth century there were, in addition to Ellen Terry, a sparkling cluster of women on the London stages. As well as Julia Neilson, Ellen Terry's sister-in-law, there were the glamorous Americans, Mary Anderson, producer as well as actress, and Genevieve Ward, an opera singer until her voice cracked and she turned to traditional drama. The young Sybil Thorndyke was just beginning to make a name for herself in Shakespeare's tragic roles, and Sarah Bernhardt could be seen in 1899 appearing as Hamlet.

This may come as a surprise to modern tastes. The decision of the Half Moon Theatre to stage Hamlet in 1979 with Frances de la Tour in the leading role caused a stir amongst the critics, for our tendency now is to let the men play men and the women play women. Frances de la Tour's interpretation of her role gave it a curiously sexless austerity, suiting the production, which sought to stress the possible political and social interferences to be drawn from the play. Such was not the intention that led to the choice of Sarah Bernhardt for the role. She was one of the last in a long English tradition which has its origins in the Restoration Theatre. Actresses at that time did not put on breeches only to appear in the scurrilous plays presented for the titillation of the gentry. They also appeared in more serious male roles. Ann, the 'matchless', Bracegirdle could be as effective dressed in men's clothes as she was in her billowing gown. The Restoration turned Elizabethan ideas of acting on their ears: no longer were boys to act the women's parts, but women were to act their own and the men's.

The result of this cross-dressing was two-fold. On the one hand there evolved the custom of principal boy in lighter productions, still frequently maintained today in pantomimes, and which can be traced to the graceful impersonations made by young Restoration actresses like Nell Gwyn. The other development was in the 'legitimate' theatre, but did not affect Shakespearian roles until the eighteenth century, when

191

72 Peggy Ashcroft as Imogen in *Cymbeline*, 1957

Sarah Siddons appeared as Hamlet in 1772. Perhaps conscious of the deleterious effect a sight of her body in male attire might have on the audience, she modestly wore a long shawl draped around her. A succession of ladies appeared as young men on the nineteenth-century stage, their costumes growing increasingly dashing and romantic. Charlotte Cushman played a pert Oberon and a languishing Romeo to her sister's Titania and Juliet. Madame Vestris, actress and manager at Covent Garden in the 1830s, was such a success in male roles that not only were souvenir pictures of her sold, but also plaster casts of her legs!

After 1900 the fashion waned, perhaps because in the wake of the Freudian stress on the importance of sexual behaviour and sexual identity, audiences felt uneasy seeing women in men's clothes. The last to perpetuate the tradition in any concentrated way was Dame Sybil Thorndyke, who played many male roles during World War II, including the Fool in *King Lear* and Ferdinand in *The Tempest*. It is significant, however, that she ceased to do so as soon as the armistice brought the male actors home from the armed forces.

The years 1945–50 also marked a general change in the style of Shakespearian acting. Sentimentality and romanticism were no longer viable after the shattering reality of war, and the younger actors and actresses aimed for naturalism in gesture and psychological realism in interpretation. For Shakespeare's heroines this produced an interesting blend of approaches. Those actresses who had trained under the old regime, like Dame Sybil Thorndyke and Dame Edith Evans, continued with the nineteenth-century style, which laid emphasis on physical grace and the beauty of the voice. These they combined with the new concentration on projecting the mind and heart of the characters they played, favoured by the younger women who appeared in the same productions with them, like Dorothy Tutin and Brenda Bruce. Some, like Dame Peggy Ashcroft, were caught between the two traditions. Not all were as fortunate or talented in adapting to current trends while retaining dignity and integrity in their acting. She combines the elusive quality of instant stage 'presence' coupled with an intuitively intelligent approach to the characters she plays.

Intelligence and subtle insight as well as the necessary acting skills, have emerged as perhaps the most significant requirements for the women who have seen their future as interpreters of Shakespeare's heroines. Since the 1950s neither directors nor audiences are satisfied any longer with a pretty face that simply mouths the words. Lillie Langtry would have a hard time at the Royal Shakespeare Company.

193

Epilogue

In the welter of words penned about Shakespeare it is rare to find comment by actors and actresses on the parts they play. No doubt this is because the significance of Shakespeare's dramatic works is assessed by literary critics, and the performances of them analysed by theatre critics, while the men and women most directly involved in bringing the plays to life are seldom asked to discuss their roles. The plays were, of course, written to be acted. There is a great deal of difference between encountering the characters in the silent pages of a book and seeing them alive on stage. When viewed by somebody actually taking part in the drama, the focus shifts again and aspects may emerge that would not occur to the mere observer.

When I spoke to four leading actresses it was clear just how enlightening the perceptions arising from this other standpoint can be. They talked to me about the Shakespearian roles they had played, and how they would interpret Shakespeare's attitude to women from the way he presents his heroines. The following are transcripts of these interviews with Brenda Bruce, Judi Dench, Glenda Jackson and Janet Suzman.

BRENDA BRUCE

Brenda Bruce became Television Actress of the Year in 1962 and joined the R.S.C. two years later. Since then she has been seen regularly on stage, film and television. Amongst her numerous triumphs, those selected for particular accolades by the critics were her portrayals of Mistress Page, Queen Elizabeth and Queen Margaret. In 1979 she gave a stunning performance as Gertrude at the Old Vic., and the production was taken on tour in Scandinavia, Europe, Australia and the Far East. During a brief return to England in the midst of this hectic tour, she very kindly granted me an interview. I first asked her how she viewed Gertrude's relationship with Hamlet:

194

BRENDA BRUCE It is a very close relationship, helped by the fact that Derek [Jacobi] and I look alike. We *look* as though we could be mother and son. Derek plays a Hamlet absolutely absorbed with his mother. It is there from the moment Claudius and I walk on and sit down. Claudius puts his hand out to me and I twine my fingers in his, before he starts to make his first speech to the council, and Derek sees that and throws himself across the stage like a child of ten. He *flings* himself into the corner. He doesn't go mooching quietly off. He can't bear it. And a little later in that scene where Claudius is saying 'Think of us as of a father' and I'm looking at him, watching this man with whom I'm newly and passionately in love, Derek's sitting on quite a low stool and he just looks up at me, just stares at me, and I don't take any notice of him at all, I'm looking at Claudius and he's looking at me. Quite often Derek cries—great tears go dropping down. Hamlet and Gertrude were terribly close and so had the capacity to hate each other very much. It's shown physically—he hits me about a lot.

ANGELA PITT What, in the closet-scene?

B.B. Yes. Understandably. It's a very passionate love/hate that we have and very violent.

A.P. Do you think it's a play about jealousy and incest?

B.B. It's a play of revenge that goes all wrong, that's for certain. He loved his father, he can't bear to think that his father was murdered. But again, the first thing he says about that is 'how could she sleep with, and make love to, this man who killed my father—I must do something about it'. Then, of course, he never has the courage. He never manages to do it. He says to his mother, 'My words will be daggers, but I'll use none'. And he does give her a terrible verbal going-over. The way that Derek and I do it is that when he has hammered on and on and on at her and finally she says 'Alas! He's mad!', she has no fear of him. She has only one moment of fear, when she says 'What wilt thou do, thou wilt not murder me?' and then he kills Polonius. From then on he attacks her mercilessly. I think that one should feel at the end of the closet-scene that if he said one thing more, Gertrude would just break into little pieces. She can't take any more, and all she can do is just remain Claudius' queen, but not his wife. It shouldn't look too easy—I mean she doesn't suddenly think 'Ugh! How disgusting!', although, mind you, if you suddenly looked at someone you were in bed with three hours ago and who in fact had killed your husband, I think you'd get a pretty violent reaction. Unless, of course, she loved Claudius over and above everything, and the answer is, in the end, that she doesn't.

195

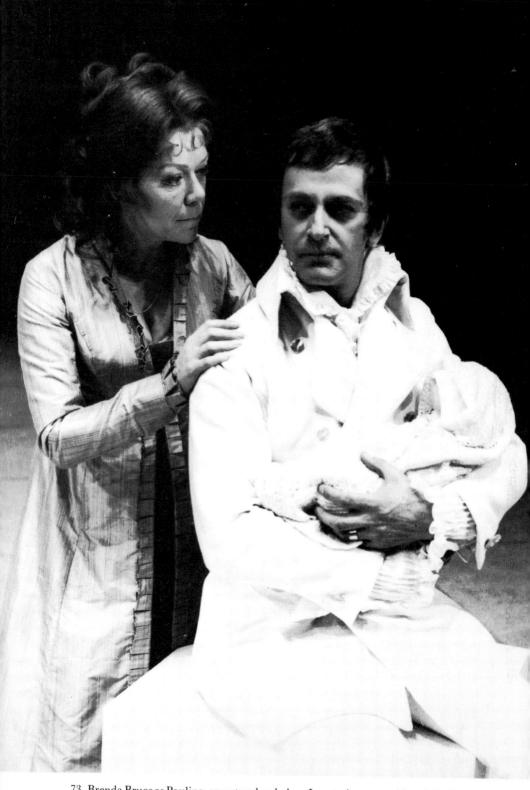

73 Brenda Bruce as Paulina, an outspoken lady at Leontes' court, and Barrie Ingham as Leontes in *The Winter's Tale*, 1969

A.P. So you play it that she does do what Hamlet suggests, and stops her sexual relationship with Claudius?

B.B. Yes, that's the way I play it. I think it works because Claudius quite often says 'Oh Gertrude! Gertrude!' and all you have to do is turn your back and leave the man alone. It's not a long part, so you've got to get an awful lot into it. Although Hamlet does a great deal of it for Gertrude—his first soliloquy, 'Frailty, thy name is woman . . .' and so on. I think he loves Ophelia, but I think he gives Gertrude a beating *through* Ophelia. Gertrude colours his whole relationship with Ophelia. When he tells her that she paints her face, for she was born with one face and she puts on another, and she lisps, and she finds nick-names for God's creatures—that's a *wonderful* speech. It's the worst of all women isn't it, that sort of 'itchy-kitchy-coo' and 'hello darling'—it's terribly modern in a way. And he's really getting at his mother. He tells Ophelia that she leads men on, and she gets them all worked up, and there should be no more marriage—'To a nunnery go!' I wanted to look rather like a nun, and I do in fact withdraw all obvious sexuality and jewellery and low-cut dresses after that closet-scene, and just go into black. But you can have so many ideas that you would end up playing her as fourteen thousand different women. I think one's just got to play a woman who at first does see that she's done wrong and is a bit uncomfortable about it, but feels that Hamlet must jolly well put up with it. I mean the 'children-can't-run-your-life, you've-got-to-have-a-life-of-your-own' sort of attitude. So at the beginning in the first scene, I don't play terribly heavily. It really is 'Look on my new husband as a friend, because that's the way it's going to be!' And when she touches Claudius, Hamlet can't bear it. She wants to convey the idea of 'Come on darling, don't go back to Wittenberg, now just *behave*, will you?' and she could kick him under the table because the court are all standing around, and when I put my hand on Derek he just freezes, he can't bear me to touch him. He's behaving disgracefully as far as she can see. Of course she knows she has married the brother and that's really not on, and married him very quickly.

A.P. 'Our o'erhasty marriage'?

B.B. Yes. But there are so many ways one could play it, as indeed with all of those women in Shakespeare. One should try—I don't mean try to get laughs, but there is a lighter side in *Hamlet*. All the stuff with Polonius. That's quite a long scene when he's saying 'Your noble son is mad!' and she's saying to him 'More matter with less art!' because he doesn't half go on! It's no good playing it terribly seriously: 'Oh he's mad! What's the matter with him?' She doesn't think he's mad, she thinks he's being frightfully *boring* and difficult, and is obviously in a very dangerous, showing-off and awful mood. Could it be love? That would be marvellous, if it's all because he's in love with Ophelia. Apart from the fact that it would make him happy and solve everything, it would let Gertrude off the hook: she needn't feel guilty then. If anybody suggests his behaviour is because she married Claudius, then of course she feels guilty. But you can't play the closet-scene in the first act. You've just got to save all that. At first you can only be an angry Mum, and quite outraged at times, and even quite funny with Polonius.

A.P. Which do you think is her best moment in the play?

B.B. I think that certainly the closet-scene is remarkable. It *can* be played as a queen being outraged by her son's behaviour, but the way I do it is that I try terribly hard not to listen, and the more I put my hands up to cover my ears, the more Hamlet knocks me about. He pulls my hands down and forces the words into my ear, and he makes love to me and he bumps me around the stage. It partly disgusts her, yet it's compelling. It is her son, and she wants to hold him because she can't bear that he is so mad—because he *is* mad by then—and that she's caused it. It's an incredible scene. When he gets me down on my knees and I say 'Thou hast cleft my heart in twain!' then we both laugh. It's an extraordinary sort of release and he says 'Throw away the worser part' and I interpret her response as 'Yes, I *will*! Now I see it! Oh that means not sleeping with Claudius, oh well I'm not sure if I can actually manage that.' And he says 'Refrain tonight'. Will she, won't she? Also, every time he walks behind me I can always sense his hand as he nearly strokes my head. I turn, but he doesn't want to be seen to do it, and so I think he's turning away from me and put out my hand, and he says 'One word more?'—that is 'Got something else to say, have you?' Gertrude just says 'What shall I do?' I'm fairly breathless by that time, because he's been banging me around and crying, and I think it is rather pathetic and childlike, really, to turn to the son and say 'What shall I do? Tell me what to do that will please you and get me out of this awful guilt.'

A.P. You find it moving to play her?

B.B. Yes. The relationship is very deep. Also the willow-speech is marvellous—that's *the* famous speech of Gertrude's. I don't think it ought to be terribly emotional. I think she tries desperately hard to do a piece of absolutely clinical reporting through clenched teeth. I don't believe one rushes in after an accident and says 'I've just seen your child! She was under a car! It's the most terrible thing I've ever seen!' It's like that for Gertrude. She goes off into other little bits, like describing the

198

74   Brenda Bruce as Gertrude and Alan Howard as Hamlet, 1970

flowers and what the naughty shepherds call them. It's her way of pro-
tecting herself and Laertes from the ghastly truth of what has happened.

A.P.   Do you do a lot of reading around a part before you take it on?

B.B.   Well, having been R.S.C.-trained, where all the directors arrive
with a huge pile of books and you're given your homework, yes, I do. I
can remember reading all the histories to find out about Margaret when
I was going to play her. One of the things I discovered, which I wanted to
do, was that she had been incredibly beautiful as a child and a girl, and
then through crying and weeping (which she did year in, year out, when
Henry was giving her such a terrible time) when she finally came back to
England, her whole face had gone like damp rot because of the tears. She
had to wear a black veil for the rest of her life. Incredible.

A.P.   Did this knowledge affect what you did in your performance?

B.B.   Well—they wouldn't let me do it. They said 'How on earth can
we do it without making a parody?' There were technical difficulties too,
as I was wearing modern dress. I wore a modern version of chain-mail
(for she was still riding and still going into battle virtually up to the end)
and wellies! So a black veil wouldn't have looked right with that!

199

A.P. You're about to appear on television in another of Shakespeare's history plays, aren't you?

B.B. Yes—as Mistress Quickly. She's very difficult.

A.P. What sort of accent do you do?

B.B. East End. That isn't difficult for me as I have a working-class background. It's just hidden away! But she's very difficult because there isn't anything to base her on in our modern life at all. She's very strange—a very strange lady, Quickly. She's terribly innocent I think. Not like Doll Tearsheet. You find women like her in any bar.

A.P. 'Innocent' seems an odd choice of word for Mistress Quickly.

B.B. Well, she gets very uppity with Falstaff, but he takes her for the most terrible rides sometimes. He says he'll marry her, and he borrows money from her and then she turns round and says 'Well, would you like to have Doll tonight?' and gets the whore along and tries to kit her out ready for a man whom she's obviously very fond of.

A.P. Don't you think there's something there that's good, that being so fond of him she's blind to his faults and blind to how she might exploit the relationship?

B.B. Oh yes. She says lovely things like 'Truer hearted man there never was!'—and he's a real bastard, he's been *foul* to her. She thinks he's so courageous and we all *know* what an absolutely dreadful coward he is. She just goes along with his own idea of himself and bolsters him up all the time. Mind you, by 'innocent' I don't mean sexually innocent. Eventually she dies of the 'malady of France'! I just feel that she is child-like in a way. It's dished out to her and she takes it. She gets frightfully cross with the servants, but when it comes round to Falstaff needing a bit more money, she gives it to him. Then he turns round and accuses her of stealing from him!

A.P. Which of the many Shakespearian characters you've played meant most to you?

B.B. Elizabeth.

A.P. Really? Why was that?

B.B. It's a better part than Gertrude. Just not as famous! Also, it's got such marvellous political stuff in it. I mean she really is in on everything that's going on. But she can't cope with all that royal bit because at first she's only Elizabeth Woodville. Not like Gertrude, who really *is* a queen.

London
12 October 1979

200

JUDI DENCH

Judi Dench is renowned for her extraordinarily sensitive and sympathetic portrayal of Shakespeare's heroines. By the time she joined the R.S.C. in 1961 she was already established as an actress of outstanding talent, having played such major parts as Ophelia, Juliet and Hermia on the professional stage. In the mid-sixties her ebullient portrayal of Viola caused a sensation. Later, much-praised roles include Beatrice and Lady Macbeth in 1976, and Adriana in 1977. Her talents have not been confined to the theatre, for in 1967 she became the Television Actress of the Year and was awarded the O.B.E. in 1970. She sets herself exacting standards, and when I met her she was deeply disillusioned with her current performance as Imogen in Cymbeline. *She spoke with wit and forceful honesty of the frustrations and delights provided by the characters of Shakespeare's women.*

ANGELA PITT   Is your interpretation of Imogen influenced by anyone else?

JUDI DENCH   No, it isn't. I try and work with a director, naturally—I need a director very very badly. Strangely enough the things I think I've probably been most successful in are the plays that I've never seen before. I think that if you're asked to *do* something, then it's an aspect of your personality, perhaps, that will be what is unique in that performance. And it may often not be right.

A.P.   Do you mean 'not be right' in terms of audience-reaction?

J.D.   Yes, it may not be right or you may never quite get the role, never quite crack the part. But it is up to you then. You've only got yourself to blame in a way. I remember seeing Peggy [Ashcroft] as Imogen and Vanessa [Redgrave] as Imogen. Both impressed me enormously, but as I couldn't possibly be either and my personality is so different from both or either of them, I just have to use what *I* have to do it. And I don't think it's right, alas.

A.P.   I'm surprised you find something wrong with it. Do you mean with your interpretation?

J.D.   Yes, but I find something wrong with it all. That's why I won't go any further with it. I only have four more performances. I talked to Peggy a lot about it and she said she found it very difficult when she played it. It is such a *monstrously* difficult part that when you come to the

201

75 Judi Dench as Viola in *Twelfth Night*, 1970

end—there are no returns or rewards. At the end I'm just terribly tired and relieved it's over.

A.P. Do you think that's Shakespeare's fault? Do you think it's a poor part?

J.D. No I don't. I think it's a wonderful part to play, but I do think it's wildly difficult. Probably the most difficult part I've played in Shakespeare and a part I never want to play again.

A.P. Why?

J.D. Well, because she's put in such unbelievable situations.

A.P. But isn't that Shakespeare's fault—that she's not credible?

J.D. I think it is credible if you do it well. For instance, when I'm lying there next to the dead body of Cloten with his head off and dressed in my husband's clothes, I always think every night, every single night, of Shaw's essay, when he says it is an unforgivable thing of Shakespeare to do, to put someone in that position. In a way that has given me enormous comfort, and from it I derive tremendous courage. I think 'Well, Shaw thought that and I think it and I'm going to battle with it and try and win'. But it's fiendish. You have to steel yourself. You don't just have to believe in that part, you have to believe beyond it.

A.P. Do you mean because it's a dimension that most people just wouldn't experience, even if it's credible in itself?

J.D. Yes. And also because now we're so used to opening our papers and watching the television and seeing the most appalling atrocities: children dying, men being shot, men just before they're shot, bodies lying on the pavement with blood streaming—we're very used to violence. Therefore if you have a very violent thing in the theatre and it is *less* than real, it stretches people's credulity. *But*, nevertheless, I'm glad I played it.

A.P. Do you now feel that you went into it naïvely?

J.D. No—I thought it was difficult, but I didn't know it was this difficult. Also I had to play her as a rebel, angry.

A.P. Her rebellion as a woman is surely one of the characteristics that make it a particularly suitable play to put on now.

J.D. Right. But she's a very feminine person, like Beatrice—a really Shavian character.

A.P. By 'feminine', do you mean using feminine wiles?

J.D. Not necessarily *wiles*, no. I mean with very female characteristics. That was what Shakespeare was so wonderful at—his understanding of not just how the 'eternal kind' of woman acts or behaves, but how a great range of women behave. You look at someone like Juliet. No one could have understood a young girl in love better than Shakespeare did. Yet you can also look at someone soured by love, like Beatrice, who is quite emancipated.

A.P. When you played Juliet, did you find the part intellectually satisfying?

J.D. Yes, for although Juliet is only fourteen years old, she is very mature, like many fourteen-year-olds today, in fact. When I played her, Zefirelli broke the mould entirely by wanting those two young people to look the age they were, so it blew that romanticism business right out of the window. He said 'Forget the poetry' which was really a heinous sin! Revolutionary. People do remember the production, which shows it was quite extraordinary. In a way, if I looked younger and could play it now, I could play it better than I did then. Now I understand about the poetry and that's what was missing.

A.P. Do you find your view of the plays is affected when you use extracts from them in verse-readings?

J.D. No, it isn't. It just means that if I've done the play I'll probably do that bit better. I mean I've never played Rosalind and I wouldn't give much shakes for the way I do the bit of *As You Like It*, because I can't attach it to anything I've been in—I haven't worked my way through that person, that character of Rosalind.

A.P. So it does make a difference when you've played the part?

J.D. Definitely. Though of course with one actor you don't reproduce what you did with another. You have to respond to the person who is speaking; it's no good just doing the same bit the same way, because people talk to you in different ways. You give the same answer in a different way because the question may be asked in a different way.

A.P. Does that apply to the performances of the plays as well? That you can give a totally different interpretation in different productions?

J.D. Yes, although not if I'm playing with the same people. For instance, when I was at the Vic., I was playing the Princess of France in *Henry V* to Donald Houston and at the same time I televised it with Robert Hardy. Different costumes, different cuts, one for the television, one for the stage, and of course, both entirely different.

A.P. Are you able to cut yourself off like that?

J.D. Yes, though the different cuts were difficult, because I'd think 'Hello, I haven't heard that bit before!' or 'That's a bit I hadn't bargained for!' So that's why everything, bad or good, is unique—and why those plays, which are so wonderful, have lasted so long. It's the *aspects* of them that change.

76 Judi Dench as Imogen in *Cymbeline*, 1979

A.P.   If Imogen is the most unsatisfactory part that you've played, what would be at the other end of the scale?

J.D.   Oh I've no idea, Angela, no idea. Did you see *The Comedy of Errors*?

A.P.   Yes—an extraordinary production.

J.D.   It was just the thing to do as a musical, all Campari and dark glasses and wonderful clothes—the men wore white suits. It was marvellous to do. I adored doing *Romeo and Juliet*; I loved *Much Ado About Nothing* and *Macbeth*. But I didn't like playing Portia. I hated the play and I hated the characters in it, and I should never have done it.

A.P.   What did you dislike about her?

J.D.   Oh, everything! I think they're all thoroughly nasty people. What a horrible way to behave! Oh, I think there's nothing to redeem them, any of them. How *dare* she behave so churlishly over that ring at the end? That's so petty—and *boring*. Oh, I *loathe* that play!

A.P.   Don't you think that it's a lesson to the audience in itself?

J.D.   I don't think it should be. I don't think you should pile them all into the theatre at Stratford and say 'You're in for a very nasty evening and you'll go out not liking any of them!' A lot of people don't like the play you know. I think the characters all behave *appallingly*, every one of them, without fail. There's nobody who behaves well. Horrible, horrible people.

A.P.   But you liked Lady Macbeth?

J.D.   Oh yes! She's all right. She sets out with all the right ideas, like an ambitious agent.

A.P.   Would you have stayed with her as her guest?

J.D.   Would I have stayed with her? I doubt that—but you never know, do you?

A.P.   No, I suppose she might have been all right to other people.

J.D.   Well, they *say* she is. They say she's the most kind hostess and Duncan gives her that lovely jewel. She can't be too bad—it's not just the cooking he gives her that diamond for!

A.P.   There are some very strange lines in that play. How did you cope with the one where she says—

J.D.   'What in our house'?

A.P.   Yes.

J.D.   Well, just in the context of it. I'm absolutely convinced it's like 'the lady doth protest too much'. If you've *done* it, the one thing you say is what people would suspect. If it's done in your house, the blame will naturally turn to you first and to your household. So the fact they *have* committed the murder means that she says the thing that is obvious in everybody's minds: that it was in her house. And everyone there is suspect. Everything is very carefully calculated at that moment. If something terrible has happened in your house, you know that the eyes of everybody are on you, whether or not you are guilty. Especially in Lady Macbeth's case as it's her cousin. It's like saying, 'Oh how frightful that such a thing could happen here!'

A.P.   Do you think that Lady Macbeth's behaviour is only valid because she's a member of the aristocracy?

J.D.   Oh no. I don't think so at all. I think you should be able to identify totally with those people when they come on. It should be 'There but for the grace of God . . . goes almost anybody'. Suddenly you should see that the ambition and greed and all the things that make up those two, makes up everybody. If you push that much greed and ambition to the limit, then terrible things can happen.

A.P.   Why couldn't you say that about—I hardly dare mention her again—Portia? That 'There but for the grace of God . . .'?

J.D.   Well indeed, I think you can. But why is it worth telling that story? It doesn't make anybody feel better at the end, does it? With *Macbeth*[1] we actually used to lock the audience in and there was no interval. Once you were on that little wheel, there was no getting off. Once those witches stepped into that circle, and Macbeth stepped in with them, there was no escape. We had a priest who came to it several times and he had a crucifix round his neck. He used to hold the crucifix up. We got to know him eventually and we said 'Are you so worried for yourself?', and he said 'No, I'm not worried for myself, I'm worried for all of you'. And that was remarkable. Sometimes there was the most extraordinary, strong feeling in that theatre. When you get people sitting in a circle, in a small room, it is something like a black Mass.

A.P.   The play certainly has the most peculiar atmosphere.

J.D.   It moves very quickly and you are caught up in it before you know where you are. And it's right that we didn't use a lot of scenery—I would never want to do it any other way.

A.P.   If we can turn to another of the tragedies—would you like to play Cleopatra?

J.D.   No, nor would I be right to. She's a sinewy 'serpent of Old Nile', and I can't see myself doing that—not at all. I could, when I was younger, have played in Shaw's *Caesar and Cleopatra*, but I can't ever see myself doing that other part. Not my cup of tea. It's not a very English role somehow. I feel that ideally she doesn't have English characteristics. There's something much more Mediterranean in Cleopatra than most of us can actually portray. It doesn't matter how much you doll yourself up and have the black hair and slink about. The only person I've seen being so uncharacteristically English was Dorothy Tutin playing Cressida. Just breathtaking. She got that mixture of being Greek, but yet being able to speak the poetry. It's a very strange thing. If you look at those women when you go abroad, they have such a different air about them, which is very difficult to reproduce. Cleopatra is a creature of that ilk. It's not just a question of snaking your hips around and being dolled up. I tried to do it in a comic way as Adriana in *The Comedy of Errors*, and so I know that the slightest thing you don't get right can give you away.

A.P.   I've never thought of dividing the women up like that, by nationalities and racial characteristics.

J.D.   Well, it helps to tell the story. It is the nearest you can get to something that is recognisable before that person opens her mouth. I think about that side more because I trained as a designer and therefore I

[1] R.S.C. performance, The Other Place, 1976.

207

know how important it is to look right. I know that it is fifty per cent of the performance. The actors don't like to hear that, but it is, there's no doubt about it . . .

London
15 November 1979

GLENDA JACKSON

Since the mid-sixties, Glenda Jackson has won international acclaim for her film performances. Amongst other honours, she was nominated The Variety Club Best Film Actress in 1971 and 1975, and has also won two Oscars. In 1978 she was awarded the C.B.E. As well as her appearances on the cinema and television screens, she has had a distinguished career in the theatre. Of the many parts she has played for the Royal Shakespeare Company, the most recent and possibly most admired, is her portrayal of Cleopatra. She generously allowed me to interview her in her dressing-room at the Aldwych Theatre while she was making-up for a performance of the play. We talked about Ophelia, her first role as a professional actress in a Shake-spearian play in 1965. I then asked about her early ambitions:

ANGELA PITT   In the sixties, did you ever see yourself becoming a Shakespearian actress to the exclusion of other types of role?
GLENDA JACKSON   No I didn't, because I'm not a person who is particularly aroused, stimulated or inspired by verse; I'm much more excited by prose usually than by verse. Even though having said that, I am at the moment appearing in a Shakespeare-play.
A.P.   With some very rich verse!
G.J.   The interesting thing though, you see, is that she has very little of the poetry, she's very practical, until the end, until that last extraordi-nary twenty minutes. It's Anthony who has all the great poetry, she doesn't. But given that it's the richness of the poetry that I find exciting, it's the richness of character embedded in a line in Shakespeare that I find thrilling. I'm not a verse-orientated person. Verse itself—I can admire it, and I can consider it beautiful and it can move me—but it doesn't feed me as an actress in the way that prose can. It's the idea of a *character* that can feed me in Shakespeare, and indeed does. Cleopatra's character is extraordinary and immensely rich and there's a hell of a lot in there, but what's in there is always for me translatable into human

208

terms; and then the whole mystic, poetic element if you like, which as a character I think she has, even if she doesn't have that much overt poetry to say, is something that comes through. But the reverse process can't work for me. There are many people in the Company for whom the actual verse has that effect, it actually stimulates their creative processes: it doesn't for me—I'm not, in that way, on an acting level, stimulated. So no, I would never have considered doing Shakespeare to the exclusion of all other playwrights, even though there are still a couple of Shakespearian parts that I would like a crack at!

A.P. What are they?

G.J. Well, I suppose they are Beatrice, in *Much Ado About Nothing*, and—really in truth, I'm a bit old now for the others, but they were Viola and Rosalind. I'm not too old for Beatrice though, and I'd like a crack at that.

A.P. You like the witty sort of woman, the ambiguous woman?

G.J. Yes. I've always found those women much more interesting than Desdemona, Ophelia, Miranda and all those fey ladies. I don't find

77 Glenda Jackson as Ophelia in *Hamlet*, 1965

them as interesting because they're not as ambiguous. There's a wonderful ambiguity about the others. I think he must have had a wonderful boy-actor when he wrote them, because there's a marvellous constant shifting between maleness and femaleness, which is not the same sort of thing as masculine and feminine at all. But the combination of mind and heart is extraordinary in those.

A.P. Do you think that Shakespeare created exciting roles for actresses? His major plays really concentrate on heroes don't they?

G.J. Yes. There is a straight line in Shakespeare for any actor of talent to go from his youth as Hamlet, to his old age as Lear, and that's an unbroken line. There's a part at every stage of a man's development. That's not true for the women. It's not true in any culture, in any society's classic theatre. I don't think that women can go through all their stages of development and have it expressed in theatrical terms. I do find it exciting to play when it's played 'not Shakespearian', which rarely happens in this country, because I do think there's been a major shift.

A.P. How do you mean?

G.J. It used to be very easy—it's not so easy now—for people to do Shakespeare and rest all their efforts solely on the fact that they were doing Shakespeare. Their contribution was that they said it beautifully. It was a tradition that it was all in the words—all you had to do was say the words and that was what it was all about. That doesn't interest me. That works well on radio and on record, when all you have is the voice. What interests me about Shakespeare is his enormous capacity for defining character, in all its ambiguous qualities and contexts. He never gives you a hint directly about the character, but if you dig, it's all there. The capacity to express character in four lines, or four words sometimes, is very thrilling. But the 'great jewel of our English Literary Tradition' doesn't interest me. They are plays—they have to be played.

A.P. Do you think you get an idea as an actress of what Shakespeare felt about women?

G.J. I think he saw them very much—well, to say 'as they are' implies that we are all exactly the same, which I don't think is true. He's a totally non-judgemental writer, which I find wonderful. He never judges: he simply puts the people *there*. I've always found his women very true in their femaleness—they are women. The thing that I find so extraordinary about Cleopatra, considering that he was writing for a boy, is that she was so female. She's none of the easy labels, because I don't think any women are, in truth. She's not just this, or just that; you can't tuck her under this label and say she's a sex symbol, or she's a virago, or she's a

78 Glenda Jackson as Cleopatra, 1978

queen—she's all those things with a very, very strong female base; in the sense that women are more practical, more realistic, all those things.

A.P. Very provocative claims!

G.J. Well I think they are. I think they're infinitely better at surviving and that is an aspect that is in a lot of his views of women. Cleopatra dies in the end—kills herself—and even the women that are killed in his plays (the obvious one that comes to mind is Desdemona), even all those fey ladies still have that truth about them: you've seen women like them. He always captures something that is essentially feminine and that is why his plays are also essentially masculine in a sense—which has nothing to do with fashion or mores—it's infinitely deeper than that. It's much more in the real roots of human behaviour and that's why I think the plays are never old-fashioned, because what he says, or the questions he asks, or the things he's looking at, are what we ask and question and look at now.

A.P. So it's not a picture of Elizabethan women, it's just women?

G.J. I don't think they're Elizabethan plays in that sense at all. There are a lot of plays that are Elizabethan and they're not nearly as interesting as Shakespeare because they're not rooted in this essential human quality—this humanity he always puts on the stage.

A.P. It's sometimes claimed by historians that in Shakespeare's women, you can get a much better picture of what Elizabethan women were like, then you can from any social documents. You wouldn't go along with that?

G.J. Oh I'm sure that's true. I'm sure there *are* things within it that were immensely topical at the time. But he was a master craftsman as well as being a genius, and obviously he would've liked an audience response that was pleasing. *Love's Labour Lost* is crammed with jokes that only an Elizabethan audience could laugh at. But underneath all that, underneath the craftsman working in a contemporary theatre, is the ability to see human beings at their most human, at their most essential and at their most basic, and that really doesn't change. The top-dressing can change and the fashions can change and attitudes can change, but the essential human-ness doesn't, and I think that he got that, incredibly.

London
24 October 1979

JANET SUZMAN

In addition to her achievements as an actress in films and on television, Janet Suzman has had a long and successful association with the Royal Shakespeare Company. Since the early sixties she has played many roles in Shakespeare's histories, comedies and tragedies. Critics have praised not only her versatility but also her charismatic performances, particularly of Rosalind in 1968–9, and Cleopatra in 1972–3. She won the Evening Standard Drama Award for Best Actress in 1973 and 1976, and the Plays and Players Award for Best Actress in 1976. With Cleopatra she broke away from the traditional concept of the part by introducing a dimension of sensual power. I was intrigued to discover how the revolutionary ideas for the role had crystallised.

JANET SUZMAN   I'd never seen a performance of the play before, so I was fresh to it—it's so rarely done. In a sense I was a little too young; most actresses come to Cleopatra at a maturer age. But we very much wanted to stress the difference in age between Anthony and Cleopatra. As far as we know from history, she died at about thirty-seven. We also wanted to get the feeling of somebody who'd been used to power from the age of eleven and to whom being a queen was as inborn as it was to Victoria, who never looked round before she sat down—the chair was always put there. We felt no time should be wasted on arguing about whether she was Egyptian or not, because clearly in the play Shakespeare wants an enormous difference between Egypt and Rome, and the theory that she was really Macedonian or something seemed neither here nor there. It's the difference between the two countries that is so important, because only in that way can Anthony's schizophrenia, his being torn in half, be really exploited. And it allowed Cleopatra to be foreign, exotic—so different from Octavia.
ANGELA PITT   But it isn't only the difference between the two, is it? Your performance also showed the tremendous strength of her character.
J.S.   That was very tied up with the idea of a woman in power. It's the only play of Shakespeare's where there is a truly reigning queen on the throne. The queens in *Richard III* for example, are retired or widowed— out of office in some way. All the plays are about male power. I felt there should be something reckless, unthinkingly commanding, about her. I also wanted to make clear that her public and private lives were very

79 Janet Suzman as Rosalind in *As You Like It,* 1968

clearly defined so that in the scenes alone with Anthony she could turn on any feminine tap she wished, but that in public, there was absolutely no doubt about who was in charge. But she's a most temperamental creature in that, for all her fantasies, she believes what she says at the moment that she says it. Totally—even if it's contradictory. People tend to get hung up about how 'feminine' it is that she should change her mind from minute to minute, but a woman who does have a very strong inner life and strong desires would believe totally in what she says at the moment that she says it, even if she changes her mind three minutes later!

A.P.   Absorbed by the intensity of the moment, and then something else may happen to change it.

J.S.   Absolutely. Totally living in the present. So those are two aspects—*real* political power, *real* status. There's also something dynastic about her, which I thought very important. There's some assurance that comes from knowing you're part of a line that goes back thousands of years. Cleopatra certainly had that. There was nothing *arriviste* or vulgar in her assumption of power—it was her due.

A.P.   I suppose it would be easy to make her vulgar on stage, so that she comes across as a tart?

J.S.   Yes—and she's not a tart, she's a very sensual creature. But the most interesting part of the play is the enigma of just how much she does love Anthony.

A.P.   Do you think it a play about hedonism—the triumph of pleasure?

J.S.   No, but it is about emotion and contrasts—we come back to the difference between living in Rome and Egypt. The Roman passion for clean lines; the clear light of Italy, the sort of fridge-like atmosphere of democracy. People sitting and discussing things in serried ranks in buildings made specially for that purpose, whereas in Egypt an absolute autocrat reigned. No strict buildings for strict debates as there were in Rome. And that shimmering light, that heat and the kind of temperament that goes with it. I don't think that temperament is manufactured. The way you sit or walk or talk; all these things are governed so much by heat, languor and the time of day. So there are all those very physical aspects of Cleopatra. A free-ranging creature. I saw no reason why her limbs should be constricted and constrained. Egyptian clothes seemed very much like Greek clothes, made for hot climates where limbs can move freely, nothing prim or prissy. I have seen photographs of earlier Cleopatra's. They were all very busty and staid and they'd always got some kind of a tiara on. Clearly the queenliness of her seemed the most essential aspect to them. But we did it in the seventies, and so the idea of what royalty was like had been knocked on the head somewhat. We wanted to show the accessible side of royalty—to 'de-statelify' her; take away that crown-on-head image. It just doesn't mean very much to us any more. It's so nice to see someone letting her hair down, literally. When it's necessary for Cleopatra to be regal, she can be. I played her as very much the queen when she asks about Octavia, about her height and her hair.

A.P.   Very different from the way she speaks to Anthony.

J.S.   Yes, although there is something else there, and it is very hard for an Anthony to do. From the very first words of the play, and there are lots of images to support this, she leads and he follows. Right up to the worst leading and following of all, where he abandons the battle and says more or less this: 'You *knew*, you *knew* that I would follow you!' And all she can say is 'O, my pardon'. The Anthony has to be—and I think it's something very difficult, especially for Englishmen—'in thrall' to her. It's such a lovely word and it's hardly used any more.

80 Janet Suzman as Cleopatra, 1972

A.P.   What, in the literal sense of being her slave?

J.S.   Yes. And Anthony is not only enthralled *by*, but in thrall *to*, Cleopatra.

A.P.   She's not 'in thrall' in the same way to him, so don't you think her suicide is partly because she's frightened she'll be humiliated in Rome?

J.S.   I think there's something else involved there. She fights like a tigress to live—she tries every which way. She arranges for the clown to bring the asps just in case there's no way out, so she's got her own final, personal solution all ready. There's some indication that Caesar really would give in to those despicable Roman practices and have:

> Some squeaking Cleopatra boy [her] greatness
> I' th' posture of a whore.

She's far too proud to bear that.

A.P.   It's strange that in a way she is *liberated* by his death. Her best poetry comes after he has gone.

J.S.   There's a wonderful turning point and I think we were the ones to discover it. It is after he's been hauled up onto the monument and dies in her arms. There's a stage direction 'she faints'. It's erroneous, but I can see why it was put in. Charmian and Iras try to rouse her and when she next speaks it's on a completely new level. She says 'No more but e'en a woman' as she realises the *smallness* of herself. To hell with being a queen or Empress. Once she realises that she's lost Anthony, she loves him better than anything else in the world. She couldn't have said 'I dreamt there was an Emperor Anthony' until he was dead, because it was only then that she realised the truth of her love for him. She only calls him 'husband' just before she dies, and she never makes that commitment before. There is a wonderful ambiguity earlier on in that play of just how much she's using him, just how much she loves him, just how much she still wants him and just how much she's politicking for Egypt. There's no doubt that she is prepared to flirt with the messenger from Caesar: she lets him kiss 'my bluest veins' and there's no doubt that she's devious. Mind you, we say that she's devious because she's a woman. If a man had been flirting with a messenger in order to get what he wanted for himself or his country, it would be called 'diplomacy'.

A.P.   The part must have made great demands upon you?

J.S.   No, it was exhilarating. There's something very special about her values, her life. The *size* of her rages, for instance when the messenger comes, is so un-English. There has always been the fascination in

England for things un-English. Exquisite combination of both despising and admiring things foreign. It's an old cliché but it's true—you just can't get all of Cleopatra because there's too much of her. She embodies everything a woman could, should or can be. Totally female. Shakespeare always writes of his women with a glowing flame of independence inside them—apart from Ophelia.

A.P.   Desdemona isn't all that independent, surely?

J.S.   She's not weak though. His women are prepared to take tremendous risks. One also gets the feeling that Shakespeare *liked* women. There are very few male playwrights about whom one could say that. They find them fascinating or frightening. You know, that Strindbergian thing where they are monsters, there to be dealt with. But Shakespeare found women moving, acceptable in their own right. He never stands in judgement.

A.P.   Have you ever found it difficult to get inside the character of any of Shakespeare's heroines?

J.S.   Yes, I was a very bad Portia. But then I can't stand Portia. There's got to be an absolute moratorium on that play! Until Portia decides to be a bit wicked, until the ring scene, it's such a long time to wait until the real girl comes out. It's hours—three hours of absolute *agony* before you can really let go and have a bit of fun. She's so po-faced—that awful recognition-scene and the casket-scenes. Awful to play. *But* it begins to pick up when she goes to Venice. Still, that's the one play I've come across in Shakespeare where I really feel that those boys must have been wonderful playing it. The effect of a stripling, a fourteen-year-old boy walking into that courtroom must have been incredible. A boy would be better than a girl every time in that play, just because of that scene. Otherwise I don't find there's much importance or anything to be got out of saying 'What if they were played by boys, how would it change?'

A.P.   He doesn't have overtly sexual encounters and perhaps that was because of the boys.

J.S.   Yes. But also there's a wonderfully exciting thing about people standing off and not actually getting to grips with each other. However, in *Anthony and Cleopatra* all such tasteful prudery seems thrown to the winds by Shakespeare. The lovers kiss at *least* three times according to the text. Cleopatra must have overpowered Shakespeare's sense of propriety—and so she should!

London
15 November 1979

218

Select Bibliography

Brown, Ivor, *The Women in Shakespeare's Life*, London, 1968

Camden, Carroll, *The Elizabethan Woman: a Panorama of English Womanhood 1540–1640*, London, 1952

Campbell, Lily B., *Shakespeare's Tragic Heroes: Slaves of Passion*, New York, 1960

Campbell, Oscar J. and Quinn, Edward G. (eds.), *A Shakespeare Encyclopaedia*, New York, 1966

Clark, Alice, *Working Life of Women in the Seventeenth Century*, London, 1919

Fiedler, Leslie A., *The Stranger in Shakespeare*, London, 1974

Figes, Eva, *Patriarchal Attitudes*, London, 1978

Gardiner, Dorothy, *English Girlhood at School*, Oxford, 1929

Gilder, Rosamund, *Enter the Actress*, New York, 1960

Granville-Barker, H. and Harrison, G.B. (eds.), *A Companion to Shakespeare Studies*, Oxford, 1966

Halliday, F.E., *A Shakespeare Companion*, London, 1964

——, *Shakespeare and his Critics*, London, 1972

Harris, Frank, *The Women of Shakespeare*, London, 1911

Kelso, Ruth, *Doctrine for the Lady of the Renaissance*, Urbana, 1956

Lloyd Evans, Gareth and Barbara, *Everyman's Companion to Shakespeare*, London, 1978

Maulde-La-Clavière, René de, *Les femmes de la renaissance*, Paris, 1878

Muir, K. and Schoenbaum, S. (eds.), *A New Companion to Shakespeare Studies*, Cambridge, 1971

O'Faolain, Julia and Martines, Lauro (eds.), *Not in God's Image: Women in History*, London, 1973

Olivier, Jacques, *Alphabet of Women's Imperfections and Malice*, London, 1617

Ranald, Margaret L. 'The Indiscretion of Desdemona', *Shakespeare Quarterly*, XIV, 1963

Reese, M.M., *Shakespeare, His World and His Work*, London, 1953

Scot, Reginald (Nicholson, B., ed.), *The Discoverie of Witchcraft ...*

wherein the lewde dealing of witches and witchmongers is notablie detected . . . , *1584*, London, 1886

Tillyard, E.M.W., *Shakespeare's History Plays*, London, 1944

Vives, Juan (Hyrde, Richard, ed.), *A very fruteful and Pleasant boke callyd The Instruction of a Christen Woman*, London, 1541

Williams, Clare (trans.), *Thomas Platter's Travels In England, 1599*, London, 1937

Wright, Louis B., *Middle-Class Culture in Elizabethan England*, North Carolina, 1935

Wright, Thomas, *Womankind in Western Europe*, London, 1869

NOTE TO THE READER

Throughout the book quotations from Shakespeare's plays are taken from the Arden Editions of Shakespeare. The only exception is *Hamlet* (as yet unavailable in Arden) where the Cambridge New Shakespeare edition has been used.

Acknowledgements

I would like to thank the following for permission to use their paintings, sketches and photographs as illustrative material for this book: The Bodleian Library, Oxford, plates 1, 6, 8, 9, 11; Joe Cocks Studio, Stratford-upon-Avon, plates 25, 36, 42, 74, 76, 78, 80; Holte Photos Ltd, Stratford-upon-Avon, plates 5, 7, 16, 26, 32, 43, 45, 73, 75; Homer Dickens, plates 58 and 59; The Shakespeare Centre, Stratford-upon-Avon, plates 4, 13–15, 17–24, 27–31, 33–5, 37–41, 44, 46–51, 54–7, 60–72, 77, 79. I am especially grateful to David Sim for the use of his photographs of *Richard III*, Plates 52 and 53. My mother, Cynthia Pitt, drew and gave me the four costume-drawings, plates 2, 3, 10, 12; I would like to record my loving thanks to her for these and for her continued encouragement.

Very special thanks must go to Brenda Bruce, Judi Dench, Glenda Jackson and Janet Suzman for their kindness in allowing me to interview them, often at times which must have been inconvenient. If there is a sense of freshness and discerning wit in this book, it comes from the conversations I had with them.

Many other people have helped to get *Shakespeare's Women* off the ground, and I must give grateful mention to: Paul Barnett, whose idea it was; James Brister, indefatigable and expert at tracking down portraits in the Bodleian; Mary Yeomans, for inside information about touring companies and the stage; Marion Pringle, Sylvia Tompkins and Mary White for their efficiency and kind assistance during the many hours I spent in the Shakespeare Centre Library. Sylvia Tompkins' help with archive-material in particular was invaluable to me. I am also immensely grateful to the editors at David and Charles: Frances Head, Anthony Lambert and especially Lydia Darbyshire, for their abundant good humour and patience over the last two years. Lastly I would like to give heart-felt thanks to Patricia Kirkham for her constructive criticism, her painstaking care in decoding my notes and emendations, and for typing the manuscript.

221

Index

Numbers in *italics* refer to plate numbers

222